POST-WAR
TIN TOYS
A COLLECTOR'S GUIDE

POST-WAR TIN TOYS
A COLLECTOR'S GUIDE

JACK TEMPEST

Wallace-Homestead
Book Company
Radnor, Pennsylvania

**To the memory of Peter
Ottenheimer of Zurich, Switzerland,
the internationally known collector
and dealer, who died tragically
in 1989.**

ACKNOWLEDGMENTS

**The author and publishers would
like to thank the following for
their invaluable help in the
production of this title:**

Klaus Banke, Wittringen, Germany
Graham Barlow, Rochdale, UK
Richard Clark, Leicester, UK
Marion and Jock Farquharson,
Forfar, Scotland
Michael Foster, London, UK
Peter Geissler, Nauheim, Germany
Christine and John Hopkinson,
Museum of Childhood, Haworth, UK
Hattie and Ross Hutchinson,
The Incredibly Fantastic Toy Show,
Lincoln, UK
Peter Jäger, Munich, Germany
Dave Jowett, Nottingham, UK
Ed Kelly, Warrington, UK
Georg Adam Mangold, Fürth, Germany
Frank Nelson, Manchester, UK
Dr Paolo Rampini, Turin, Italy
Jim Roberts, Woolacombe, UK
Jim Whittaker, Bamford, UK
Ankie and David Wild,
Ribchester Museum of Childhood,
Preston, UK

A QUINTET BOOK

First published in the United States by
Wallace-Homestead, a division of the
Chilton Book Company, Radnor, Pennsylvánia.

ISBN 0-87069-632-7

This book was designed and produced by
Quintet Publishing Limited
6 Blundell Street
London N7 9BH

Creative Director: Terry Jeavons
Designer: James Lawrence
Project Editor: Judith Simons
Photographer: Ian Howes

Typeset in Great Britain by
Central Southern Typesetters, Eastbourne
Manufactured in Hong Kong by
Regent Publishing Services Limited
Printed in Singapore by Kim Hup Lee Printing Co. Pte. Ltd.

Contents

Introduction

Children have always felt the need to play with toys. Though it took centuries for tinplate toys to arrive on the scene, they commanded the stage for only a relatively brief period of time before disappearing from the world markets, to be replaced by examples manufactured from modern plastics.

Primitive toys were an amalgam of easily obtainable materials – wood, pebbles, and contemporary fabrics. Metal toys came later; perhaps they were at their most popular in the form of. toy soldiers – still appreciated by children of all ages. The very wealthy could afford to have their minuscule regiments specially created from precious metals; the poorer had to be content with wooden versions. The mass-produced "tin" soldiers which eventually dominated the field were really lead-molded figures and should not, therefore, be classified as tin toys. The same holds true for the diecast metal automotive and figural toys currently collected and still being manufactured in quantity today.

THE EMERGENCE OF TINPLATE TOYS

Nuremberg, in Bavaria, had become the historic center of the toy industry many years before the word "toy" came to be used to describe children's playthings. Toys, originally, were miniature items of curiosity or usefulness, such as accessories used in sewing and embroidery. It was possibly Nuremberg's pewter trade which founded the tinplate toy industry for which the town was to become eventually renowned.

This 4½in/12cm-tall British-made clockwork-powered novelty toy features a clown with a dog swinging from his walking stick. It still retains its original box, but neither box nor toy carries any clue as to its manufacturer. It probably dates from the 1950s to '60s.

2

This 12½in/32cm-long model of a Porsche sports car features a visibly sparking engine; it was made by Rico of Spain in the 1960s.

2

3

This colorful mechanical walking "Esso" tiger, carrying a bunch of flowers, was produced in Japan for the American toy company, Marx. Dating from the 1960s and 8in/20cm tall, the tiger's tinplate body is realistically finished in striped fabric; the head is plastic.

"Tin" toys — actually manufactured from sheet iron plated with a protective layer of tin to prevent rusting — achieved their great international thrust with the onset of the mass-production methods introduced by the Industrial Revolution in the 18th and 19th centuries. Prior to this, tin toys had been stamped out and molded by hand-operated devices, and then decorated by hand. Powered machinery meant that production could be stepped up and output increased. The invention of chromolithography — the production of colored prints by lithography — also helped to speed up the process, once offset printing had solved the difficulties of printing onto sheet metal. Soon Nuremberg products were pouring out of Germany and flooding the markets of the world. Other local firms joined in, making Germany the toy supplier of the world.

German products generally began to upset world economy in a way similar to today's domination of world markets by Japan. Commercial toymaking in other

3

7

countries began as a planned response to check German imports. In the 1920s and '30s Japan itself exported a number of tinplate mechanical toys which were noted for their cheap prices, a fact often reflected in their quality. A number of American tinplate manufacturers produced excellent mechanical toys, although heftier and larger sheet-metal and cast-iron toys in particular enjoyed a popularity in the United States almost unknown on the other side of the Atlantic.

Recycling of materials was nothing new, even in the turn-of-the-century years, when industry often relied on local families as outworkers. The toymakers of France and Germany would use tinplate material scavenged from rubbish dumps. Many Japanese toys, even in the 1930s,

were made from recycled food cans, the original labeling printed on the tin still being visible on the inside of the toy!

Tin toy manufacturing in other countries also came as a result of the shortages caused by the outbreak of World War I. Light-engineering businesses on both sides of the battlefield had been taken over to tackle the more important business of providing munitions and other essential operations. When peace returned, in 1918, many firms in the Allied countries capitalized on German incapacity by attempting to take over the market in dolls, toys and other playthings. Overall, they were not too successful and, within a few short years, Germany had regained its old lead as the main producer of tin toys to the world. Their toys were

4

The "Mystery Car," produced by the German company Neuhierl in the 1950s, came with a special garage fitted with a door at either end. The mystery is the way the clockwork car exits through one door, hugs the garage wall, and returns via the back door. The car's streamlined body and slightly offset front wheels keep it traveling forwards, although gently pressing against the garage wall as it slowly moves along.

4

well made, innovative, and sold at a reasonable price. They managed to dominate the world's toy markets up to the outbreak of World War II.

THE POST-WORLD WAR II SCENE

Germany was not only defeated in World War II – the country was also fated to lose its domination of the world's toy industry. War once again put a stop to toymaking and all other non-essential industries in the countries involved militarily. When peace returned in 1945, manufacturers had a great deal of lost ground to recover. The main problem facing toymakers, in common with most other industrialists, was the shortage of raw materials. Some of the toys marketed

5

5
This small (3in/8cm-high) tinplate somersaulting monkey is marked "Made in US Zone." It is evidently German-made and dates from the 1950s when the Americans still occupied Germany's main toymaking area around Bavaria. The actual identity of the manufacturer is uncertain.

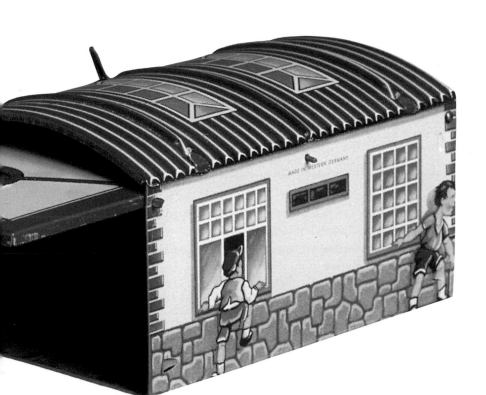

in the early years of peace had actually been made just prior to, or in the very early days of, the outbreak of hostilities. These toys had survived the destruction of war safe in storage and could now find plenty of customers – there was much demand following years of deprivation and rationing.

The Allies occupying the defeated countries of Germany and Japan encouraged a return to manufacturing by giving financial aid to the countries' industries. Toymaking recommenced in Germany, especially in Bavaria which was in the American sector. Up to the 1950s, tin toys produced there usually carried the words "Made in the US Zone." Similarly, Japanese toys of the immediate post-war years were marked "Occupied Japan." Some collectors specialize in collecting toys carrying these legends. Before long, however, toys once again carried the name of their country of origin. Japan resumed its pre-war style "Made in Japan," but Germany now used "Made in West Germany," in deference to its new position as a divided country. The old familiar patent mark "DRGM" (Deutsches Reich-Gebrauchsmuster) was changed to "DBGM" (Deutsches Bundes-Gebrauchsmuster).

However, once the toy industry was back in full production, it was the Japanese who began to flood the world market with many wonderful tin toys. By now, Japanese toys were produced to a much higher standard than their between-wars output. They were also appealingly designed, generally having ingenious actions. Besides clockwork and friction-operated toys, Japanese factories produced many novelties which were electrically powered from dry batteries. These Japanese toys could, therefore, be provided with flashing lights and loud noises, including siren and whistle sounds. They could even be given the power of speech!

These two small (5½in/14cm-long) Japanese-made tin toys are marked "Occupied Japan" and therefore date to the late 1940s to early '50s, the era before the Americans quitted Japan following World War II. Both clockwork-powered, the first example depicts a tinplate walking horse with a celluloid rider, and the second a "fairy-tale" mounted soldier towing a cannon.

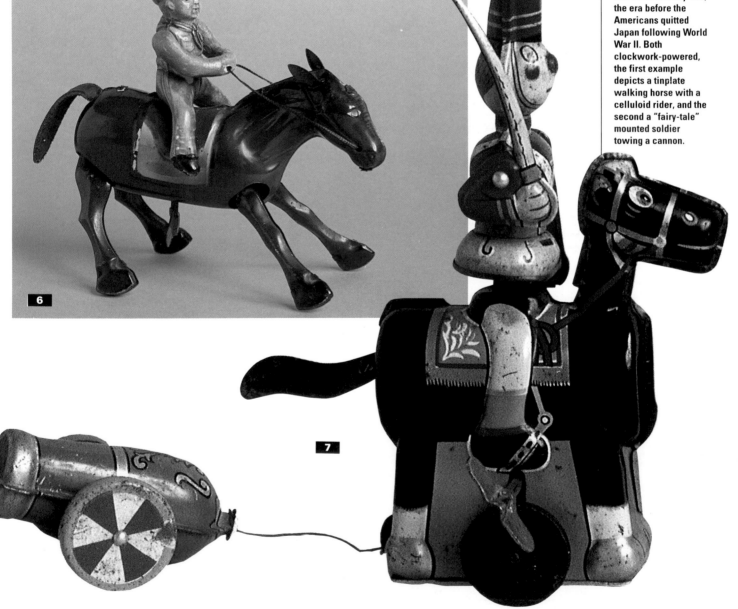

8

This "Grand Prix Racer" by Yonezawa is, at 17in/43cm long, one of Japan's larger toys from the 1950s. Solidly made, it has three gears – forward, reverse, and neutral – operating the electric motor which powers it. It makes realistic engine noises, too, and has a few flashing lights for novelty effect.

The great bulk of the Japanese toy output was aimed at the United States and its "almighty dollar." Product design often confirmed this – there were American police cars, limousines, and the commonest battery toy figure of all, "Charlie Weaver." This toy bartender figure is known in most countries, although only the Americans are familiar with him as an early TV personality.

8

9

The driver of this 10in/25cm-long battery-operated vehicle wants to say "hello" to everyone, turning his head and raising his hat to passers-by as he travels along. Hence the name "Hello Car" printed on its original box. Produced by Nomura Toys in the 1950s, this is an excellent example of quality post-war toymaking by the Japanese.

Despite this initial resurgence in tin toy production, the post war period was destined to prove a bad one for the toy industry in general. Toymakers were faced with steadily increasing production difficulties brought about by a number of factors – changing consumer demands, competition between the Western and Eastern industries, and the approach of the economic depression which affected industry in general by the late 1970s. Even the Japanese dramatically reduced their toy output, while many big names, such as Schuco in West Germany, Marx in the United States and the United Kingdom, and Meccano in the UK, ceased production altogether.

Very few tin toys are produced today. Manufacturers have found that molded modern plastic materials are more economical and cheaper to pack and

9

10 — 12
The two jeep-style military vehicles are pure novelty toys which offer amusing erratic mechanical action. They were manufactured by Marx of the United States in the 1950s to '60s. The US Army truck was made in the 1950s also by Marx.

10

11

12

13
This present-day 9½in/ 24cm-long "Passenger Plane" is fitted with friction-drive. Chinese toys of this type are generally of good quality.

14
Of fairly recent Japanese manufacture, dating to the 1970s to '80s, space-fantasy buffs will be attracted by this strange, colorful space vehicle known as "MS 134." It is powered by clockwork, has a whirling, sparking disc propeller on top, and is 8½in/22cm long.

transport. Moreover, new safety regulations forbade toys with sharp edges and open clockwork mechanisms which could easily cause injury to a child, and the use of paint containing a high lead content. The cost of producing tin toys that complied with such codes of safety proved prohibitive – the use of plastic was the obvious alternative.

Some tin toys are still produced in the Far East, although Japan no longer dominates the market. For a while China assumed that role. Primitive tinplate toys are produced in India, but they are very crude and poorly made. Examples are often found as curiosities among collections, introduced privately by their collectors, but they would never be allowed an import licence for commercial sale in most Western countries.

Collecting Post-War Tin Toys

"Post-war" and "pre-war" to collectors always refers to World War II (1939–1945). Earlier toys produced either side of World War I (1914–1918) are always referred to more specifically – "It's pre-World War I" or "It dates from just after the first World War" are phrases commonly used to describe a toy from the earlier part of this century. Thus a post-war tin toy is one that appeared on the market any time from the 1950s up to more recent years.

Tin toys are not always solely composed of tinplate. As has been seen in the introduction, tin gave way to modern molded plastic in response to demands for economy and stringent safety regulations. However, this was a slow process

and many toys during the transition period were part tinplate, part plastic in their make-up. Tin toy collectors accept the use of a reasonable amount of plastic, as this material appeared on many post-war tin toys – as ladders on fire-engines, as figures depicting passengers or drivers of vehicles, and other such accessories.

15

This is a comical mechanical tractor toy from the British firm of Mettoy, produced in the 1950s. It is 6in/15cm long and has a frantic, "Whoopee Car" type of action.

15

17
This is "Dapper Dan" at the wheel of his 5½in/14cm-long novelty inertia-powered "old-time" car, which is equipped with "mystery action" designed to push it away from solid objects blocking its progress. An amusing toy, it was made in the 1960s by Kanto of Japan, at a time when the heads of figures were still being formed from tinplate; later it was found to be more economical to mold them from vinyl plastic.

16
Battery power motivates this 10in/26cm-long "Magic Bulldozer" – an example of tinplate engineering from a period when even the drivers were formed from tinplate and not plastic. This driver grapples with the controls as the vehicle moves around with flashing lights in the engine, its "bump-and-go" mechanism turning it away from any obstacle that lies in its path.

THEME COLLECTING – BATMAN

Some collectors have a specialized interest in one particular type of toy: it might be motor vehicles in general, or motor vehicles of a particular marque, or it might be a collection of toys based on a character figure as shown here. Batman associated tin toys are possibly the most collectible of all the many fantasy playthings which have been marketed since the 1950s. The way-out adventures of Batman, not forgetting his fearless sidekick Robin, the Boy Wonder, first appeared as strip cartoons and, as their fame as the crime-busters of Gotham City spread, their fight against numerous picturesque "baddies" was transferred to the cinema and TV screens.

Avid Batman collectors do not draw the line at collecting tinplate toys and are happy, too, to acquire examples of their hero's memorabilia fashioned from plastic – or any other material, for that matter. The accompanying illustrations from a leading collection show the range of such toys manufactured only from tinplate. Other Batman based toys, including a hoop-la game, machine gun, and a spinning top can be seen in the chapter on Other Tinplate Toys.

19
Although called "Batman" on its box, this toy has an unusual Batmobile design. It was made by Yanoman Toys of Japan in the 1960s, and is 6½in/16cm in length. It features Batman, without Robin, in the driving seat.

22
This "Batmobile" toy was manufactured following a takeover of Aoshin in 1972. Again it has powered lights, and the push-away "mystery action" common to many Japanese-made toy vehicles of the post-war years.

18
This fine tinplate walking Batman, powered by clockwork, was issued to commemorate the 1989 *Batman* movie and has become an instant collectible. It is made by Biliken of Japan, and is 8½in/22cm tall; a mechanical Joker figure was brought out by Biliken at the same time.

21
Aoshin (trademark "ASC") made this friction-drive "Batmobile" for the Japanese home market in 1966; the writing on its box is entirely in Japanese. It is 11in/28cm long and features Batman without his trusty sidekick, Robin.

19

20
This is the rare version of the Aoshin 1966 friction-powered "Batmobile" and was produced at around the same time. This model – again featuring a lone Batman – is 8½in/22cm long and battery-operated by remote cable control; the batteries are positioned in the tinplate controller unit and not in the vehicle itself. This was the first remote-controlled Batmobile toy to be produced.

21

20

22

23

23
Batman memorabilia is here represented by miniature American-style automobile license plates, manufactured in Hong Kong in the mid 1960s for Marx of the United States. They are 4in/10cm in width and perfectly preserved in their original polyethylene sealed bags.

25
This 13½in/34cm-long battery-operated "Batmobile" was made in Japan by Aoshin in 1966. The rare black version is illustrated here; a blue version of the toy was issued by Aoshin from 1968 to 1972.

24

25

24
This tin friction-drive "Batplane" was made in Argentina in the 1950s and is 10in/26cm in length. It is marked "Copyright National Periodical Publications Made Under License," but carries no trademark or maker's name.

26
This is a 12in/31cm-long battery-operated blue "Batmobile" from Taiwan, made in the 1970s to '80s. It is known as the large "Piston Batmobile" because of its exposed engine mechanism at the rear.

26

27
This red battery-powered "Batmobile," made in the 1970s to '80s, is 12in/31cm in length and carries a logo of a black cat, the trademark of Cien Ge Toys of Taiwan. The vehicle produces sounds reminiscent of a jet engine and has blinking lights.

27

28
An example of a toy manufactured from several materials, the main parts of this cycling boy and dog are tinplate, but the bicycle wheels are hard plastic and the boy's head is of vinyl. This is a clockwork-driven Japanese toy of indeterminate make, 5½in/14cm in length, dating from the 1950s.

28

29
A toy for the circus and fairground enthusiasts, this 5½in/14cm-long "Coney Island Scooter" is a bumper-style car with inertia drive. It is marked with the name of an American toy producer, "Flare Import Corporation New York Copyright 1962," and also carries the "KO" trademark of Kanto Toys of Japan. The figure's head is molded from vinyl.

Post-war toys are usually less expensive than their earlier counterparts, though certain items realize quite high prices when they appear in auction sales. A few years ago post-war toys were not considered very desirable, but the shortage of the classic pre-war tin toys — and their correspondingly high prices — have turned collectors' attentions towards the previously neglected toys of the 1950s and after. At present, without doubt among the most valuable of these toys are the highly collectible tinplate robots which came from Japan in the 1950s and '60s, and also any of the wonderfully produced tinplate models of the exotic American limousines of that particular period. The West Germans also issued similar model cars which are today equally highly valued and eagerly sought after.

WHERE TO BUY

There are many toy enthusiasts who are happy to buy, sell, or exchange items. They operate from their homes and, more often than not, are to be met as

29

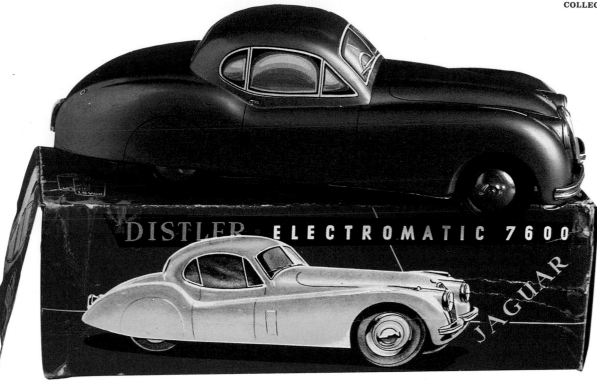

30

30

Manufactured in the 1950s by the German firm of Distler, this "Electromatic 7600" toy is a 8½in/22cm-long model of a X120 Jaguar car. It is battery-operated and boasts two forward gear speeds and one reverse. A beautiful tinplate pressing shows no crease marks.

31

stallholders at the various specialist toy fairs or collectors' swapmeets. A few of them run small shops or carry out their business from antique centers. The majority of these people are usually collectors in their own right. They are useful to know, as they can often be of service in discovering items sought by a particular client. Their advice and knowledge can also be helpful in identifying items. Some offer a reliable restoration service for neglected tin toys, or are able to recommend an expert in this field.

Fairs themselves can vary enormously. Many display a mixture of diecast and tin toy collectibles, usually with diecast automotive models predominating. Other types of juvenilia may also be displayed. Some events may include dolls; while on the other hand, doll fairs often feature the odd stall or two which specializes in old toys. General toy stalls are often found at many larger collectors' fairs and flea-markets.

Toys are also bought privately, often as a result of placing a small advertisement

Space toys hold a special appeal to many collectors and this 1950s futuristic monorail toy is a rare example, produced in early post-war Japan by Nomura of Tokyo. The track forms a loop and the 10in/25cm-long rocketship-style vehicle runs along by battery power, and features an illuminated headlight.

31

32

"Haggling" is a custom at these events and even non-English-speaking buyers seem to be able to ask for the "best price." Collecting toys is an international interest today and the better known toy fairs in every country can expect at least one or two foreign collectors as visitors, if not as stallholders. Most prices tend to be negotiable – the vendor may often be offering a slightly higher price in anticipation of bargaining!

Where the Fairs Are

A list of toy fairs from various countries is contained in the appendix. The listing does not include every known toy show. New events keep appearing on the scene quite frequently, while some of the less successful shows are liable to disappear suddenly without trace. It would also be impossible to include full details – as well as dates and detailed addresses – in a book like this, as the situation is constantly changing. However, there are many magazines which contain updated toy show details. In the United States, for instance, *Collectors' Showcase*, the *US Toy Collector Magazine*, and *Toy Shop*, all carrying lists and advertisements for future fairs. In Germany there are listings in the magazines *Puppen & Spielzeug* and *Sammler Journal*; in the UK *Collectors' Gazette* is the best source of such information.

CONDITION AND AUTHENTICITY

The standard to aim for in acquiring items for any collection is "mint." This means that the toy looks as new as the day it left the factory where it was manufactured. Whether it has its original box or not is immaterial in the case of tin toys; with diecast toys, where battered items can easily be made to look like new, the presence of an original box is a kind of insurance that the article is genuine. In general, tin toys do not suffer the same attentions from fakers, though quite a lot of "restoration work" goes on in the trade. Thus it is essential to get the "feel" of the real thing. Restoration should be left to the experts and any amateur attempts avoided at all costs. A good dealer will inform a client if the toy he is

in the local newspaper. It is surprising how many items still turn up from such sources. Even personally unwanted examples may be useful to acquire, to be swapped later for more interesting pieces.

Minding a Stall

Taking a stall at one of the toy fairs is a good way of being admitted to a show before the general public. Much wheeling and dealing takes place before the doors are officially opened. There is also the chance of being able to buy from members of the public, who often bring in interesting items to offer to the traders.

At the more popular events it is usually necessary to reserve a place well in advance of the advertised date. In many cases the organizer already has a waiting list, such is the demand for stalls at the shows which tend to attract the largest crowds. The rental charge is usually based on the use of a two-yard (two-metre) long folding table or its equivalent, the fee increasing accordingly if more than one table is required. Some shows allow traders to erect extra small tables which they have brought with them, others do not. It is best to find out the show's ruling in advance.

32

This unusual tinplate clockwork circus carousel, 11½in/29cm in diameter, carries the trademark "JML" and was made in France, probably in the 1960s to '70s. The figures are actually made of hard plastic and the toy carries the name "Lugdunum Circus."

33

Americans in particular liked the type of toy they call the "Whoopee Car;" if they did not invent it, then they certainly adopted it. This type of vehicle has a clockwork mechanism and gearing designed to make it jerk rapidly backwards and forwards, much like a bucking bronco, throwing its pivoted driver all over the place! This toy, known as the "Crazy Jeep" and a mere 4½in/11cm in length, is a product of the English firm of Graham Bros, trading under the name "Fairylite." It was produced c 1950.

selling is original or otherwise – at least, he should inform the client of any restoration work that has been carried out.

Restored items may lose some of their original charm, no matter how well the task has been carried out. While "do-it-yourself" workmanship can prove dangerous if performed by the inexperienced, the charges of the professional restorer can be quite high. It is as well to remember that this added expense may not be easily recoverable if it becomes necessary to sell the toy.

While the desired aim may be for a collection of mint condition toys, the collector must be prepared to accept toys of inferior quality. Mint examples are always thin on the ground and, in any case, it is hardly realistic to expect toys to remain in pristine condition when they have been played with by children. The majority of toys which have survived in perfect condition have usually been discovered safely stacked away in factory or shop storerooms. The condition of those others which have been in circulation depends upon the kind of treatment they received at the hands of their original young owners, as well as the environment in which they have survived the years. A dry attic is one thing, but tin toys suffer when they lie forgotten for a few years in a damp outbuilding or garage.

34

FINDING OUT ABOUT TIN TOYS

A visit to the local reference library will be most helpful, though the majority of books will deal mainly – some solely – with pre-war tin toys. But there are several volumes which include information about the post-war varieties; see the Bibliography at the back of this book for some recommendations. Old trade catalogs and advertising pamphlets also contain a great deal of useful information, often helping to date items – many collectors like to include such ephemera among their works of reference. They make a nice side-collection in their own right, and can turn up in the most unlikely places. They usually command reasonable prices, though they can be relatively expensive when offered at an auction sale. Discarded mail-order catalogs also offer a useful source of information.

34

Fascinating in its simplicity, this comical tin toy from Toplay of Japan features a black boy using a bunch of bananas to tempt his hippo steed along its way. It is 6in/15cm long, clockwork, and dates from the 1950s to '60s.

35

This 5½in/14cm-tall, brightly colored and well-made clockwork marching soldier offered quite a bit of amusement value for its low price when it was marketed by Toplay of Japan in the 1960s to '70s.

33

35

Tinplate Figures

Animated tinplate figures are direct descendants of the wonderful pieces of automata which only the very rich could afford in past centuries. Although necessarily much smaller and a great deal simpler in their actions, they nevertheless possess a great deal of special charm. And, as ever, performance is intrinsically linked with quality.

Then the Japanese – who had been noted for economically made pre-war toys – began to flood the markets with a magical array of attractively turned-out quality toys which impressed the toy-buying world. There were tin toy animals dressed in human clothes, which ran along powered by clockwork, playing drums, reading books, chasing balls, spinning propellers on their noses, and attempting all kinds of acrobatics; some drove cars or rode on motor cycles. Many

37
Sweet-toothed "Candy Dog," made in Japan in the 1950s, does nothing but eat sweets; he empties one from his candy tin into his left paw and scoops it into his mouth. By a miracle of mini-automation the sweet is returned, unseen, back to the tin for recycling! This fascinating clockwork toy with no maker's mark, is 6½in/16cm tall.

38
This fabric-covered tinplate toy, designed and produced by Alps Shoji of Japan, is entitled "Lazybones – the Sleeping Pup." It is a 9in/23cm-long figure of a lounging hound with a wasp on his toe. The wasp buzzes while the dog regards it with mild amusement, waggling his foot a little in a lazy attempt to scare the creature off, yawning and blinking his eyes as he does so. This delightful clockwork toy, dating from the 1950s, is extremely hard to find nowadays.

36
An interesting 1950s clockwork novelty toy from GAMA of Germany, the monkey performs acrobatics as the motorcycle travels along; 6½in/17cm in length.

CLOCKWORK FIGURES
The attraction of these movable toys is an amalgam of appearance and the ability to perform fascinating movements. The best of the tinplate novelties were made by the Germans prior to the outbreak of World War II, but the situation altered after the war. Old-established German toymakers, such as Lehmann, GAMA, and Schuco were soon back in the export business. For a good few years, they turned out an interesting number of novelties without, however, quite recapturing their old mystique. New production methods did not result in products which matched their old flair.

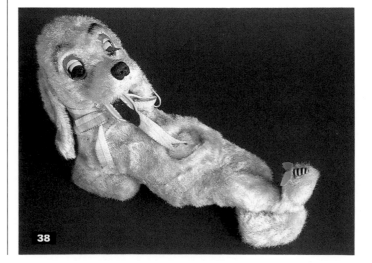

39

This 1950s toy by Toplay of Tokyo represents a basketball-playing monkey. This clever toy demonstrates the accuracy of the tinplate monkey's throw as he safely lands the ball into the net, from which it is returned to him for a repeat performance – and so on, until the clockwork motor needs rewinding. It is 7½in/19cm long.

40 **41**
Made in Japan during the 1950s (manufacturer uncertain), these two toys are very similar; one is finished to represent a young boy and the other a bear. They have clockwork motors and appear to be reading their books, flipping over the pages one by one by means of a small magnet hidden in the right hand – or paw. They are around 6½in/17cm tall.

40

41

42

43

43
Many little mechanical clockwork toys like this came from Japan in the post-war years. They are certainly made from tinplate, although covered in suitable fabric to imitate the animals' natural appearance. Here we have a hungry rabbit – its action never allowing it to stop eating, at least until it needs winding up again! The manufacturer is uncertain; it is 5½in/14cm tall.

42
This German-made toy (manufacturer uncertain) presents the same basic monkey in two different ways. The smaller (3½in/8.5cm-tall) version ambles along looking as though he is going to bowl a ball which he holds in his right hand. The larger toy (6in/15cm high) features the same monkey perched on a plastic wheel. This contains a clockwork mechanism which moves the toy alternately backwards and forwards.

44
This unusual acrobatic 1950s toy is by Toplay of Japan. The 5in/13cm-high tin monkey dangles from a suspended string and mechanically works his way along from one end to the other.

45
The 3in/7cm-tall clockwork bear climbs the pivoted ladder which gradually tips with his weight, gently lowering him to the ground. This is an unusual British novelty toy by an unknown maker, produced in the 1950s to '60s.

44

45

such toys appeal to enthusiasts of differing interests and can equally find their way into collections of, say, novelty toys and road vehicles – a fact which, unfortunately, can help to inflate the value of an item.

Circus toys are always eagerly sought after, combining bright cheerful coloring and rapid movement. There are clowns in abundance, some playing instruments, somersaulting, pushing barrels along, swinging by their arms, and walking on their hands. One nice example from the 1960s, made by TPS of Japan, features an elephant pulling along a series of three acrobatic clowns, all showing off their skills as the procession travels along.

In the post-war years, many German firms concentrated on clockwork rather than battery-operated animal figures. The firm of Köhler was particularly noted for its small, but well-produced, tinplate toys featuring cats and dogs. The Köhler cat with ball was much imitated by other makers, sometimes in a slightly larger scale. Examples include products of the American firm of Marx and several Japanese toy manufacturers.

Examples of clockwork figures also come from other countries, as well as Japan and Germany. Unique Art, in the United States, made an appealing character called "GI Joe & His K-9 Pups"

46
This is a real piece of 1950s tinplate mini-automata, made in Japan by Toplay. Simple in action yet ingenious, this 5½in/14cm-high clockwork "Animal Barber Shop" represents a mouse barber giving a rabbit a shave.

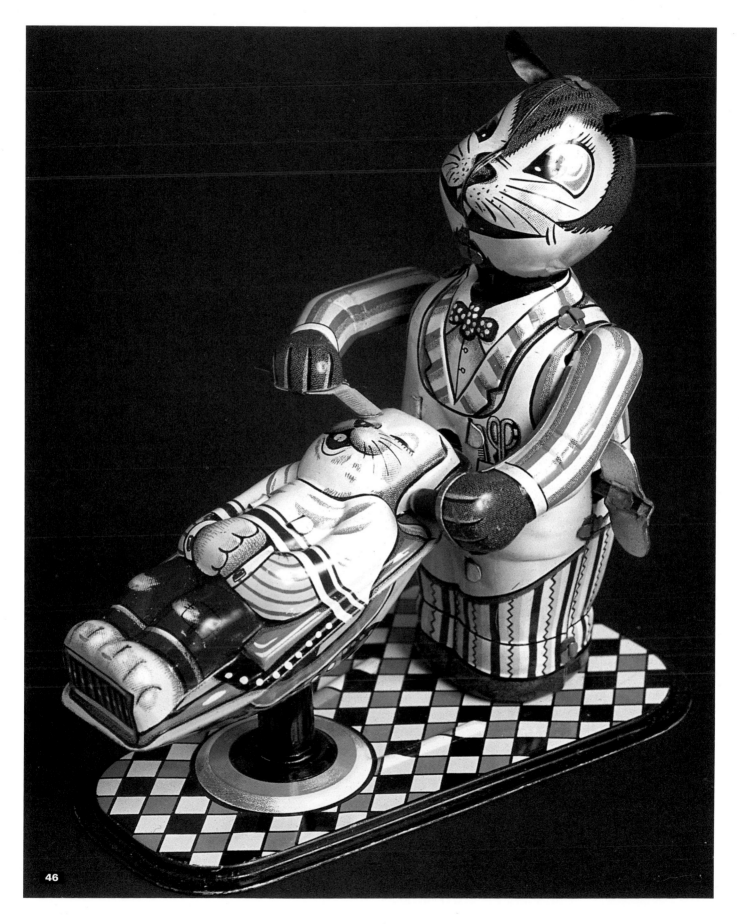

CLOCKWORK CIRCUS TOYS

47

"Violin Clown" fiddles away frantically, but unfortunately produces no music. He is 6in/15cm tall and wobbles precariously as he plays away, thanks to his clockwork mechanism. This appealing 1950s toy was produced by an unknown Japanese maker.

47

48

48

"Hobo Clown" was produced by Linemar Toys of Japan in the 1950s and closely resembles the firm's noted "Popeye Skater" (see the chapter on Character Toys). Both toys are identical in size (6½in/16cm tall) and in their clockwork action.

49

A fascinating toy produced by Nomura Toys of Japan in the 1950s, "Circus Boy" moves around, shaking his head from side to side, and flourishes a circus poster while ringing a handbell. The clockwork-powered toy is 6in/15 cm high.

49

50

50

This delightful mechanical Japanese toy, produced by Toplay in the 1950s, features a clown holding a "fiery" hoop through which a dog leaps as the hoop circles around. The toy is 6½in/17cm tall and the "fire" is represented by red felt.

51

51

This 1950s British-made tin toy features a clockwork clown climbing a wooden pole. Ingeniously made and nicely finished, no maker is credited, even on its original box. The clown is 4½in/12cm tall.

52

53 "Bozo the Clown," a mechanical clockwork drummer from Alps of Japan, is a finely made colorful tin toy of the 1950s, produced before plastic materials made inroads into toy production. Bozo is 8½in/21cm tall.

54 This simple 1950s tin clockwork clown precariously walks along on his hands, hence the name "Inverted Clown" donated by its British maker, Wells-Brimtoy. It is 5in/13cm tall.

54

55

52 "Good Time Charlie," 10in/26cm tall, is a jolly clockwork clown from Alps Shoji of Japan, which blows a noisy party-squeaker. He is actually formed with a minimum of tinplate: the fabric of his clothing hides a cardboard body and his head is molded from composition material. However, the majority of tinplate collectors would be happy to include Charlie among their toys. This toy should not be confused with the Japanese battery toy of the same name in the form of a top-hatted inebriate.

53

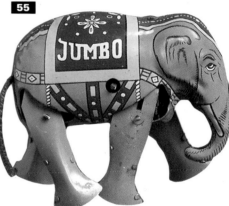

55 This clockwork walking tinplate elephant is named "Jumbo" and was made in the early 1950s by Lesney Products of the UK, when they briefly entered the tinplate market before concentrating on the well-known diecast vehicles produced under the names "Matchbox Toys" and "Models of Yesteryear." Lesney's "Jumbo" is an almost exact copy – even to its height of 4in/10cm – of the elephant produced by Blomer & Schüler of Germany, which had proved such a best seller that the German firm honoured it by adopting the elephant as its trademark, together with the initials "B&S."

56 This clockwork-powered toy represents a clown riding a motor cycle who appears to be oblivious to the antics of the monkey which leaps on and off the pillion seat. The toy measures 6½in/16cm in length and was produced in the late 1950s by Kanto of Japan.

56

57
This "Drummer Boy" was a popular tinplate toy figure issued by Marx in the United States during the 1950s and '60s. He stands 9in/23cm tall and a clockwork mechanism produces the drumbeats.

58
This "Trumpet Player" toy is clockwork-powered and was made in the 1950s to '60s by Nomura Toys of Japan. He is 10in/26cm tall and sways around like a real trumpet player – even producing an attempt at a trumpet sound, although many examples have lost this ability over the years.

59
This Japanese "Talking Parrot" by Asakusa Toys is a neat little novelty from the 1950s to '60s era. The parrot – 8½in/21cm tall, including the perch – does not actually talk, but can produce a few meaningless sounds!

which would walk along when the clockwork motor was wound. He was prevented from falling over by the two baskets holding the lithographed puppies he was carrying, which trailed along each side of his feet. The American firm of Chein produced a number of fascinating tin toys, including a waddling duck. An interesting ringmaster and prancing horse toy, issued for a brief period in the late 1940s by Arnold of West Germany has proved very collectible, especially by circus-toy enthusiasts.

An ingenious tin toy featuring two sparring boxers was produced by Biller of West Germany in the 1950s. A very similar toy was sold in the UK, and marked "Made in England." It may have been a copy, or had perhaps been ordered from Biller by a firm of distributors. In the 1960s Rico of Spain issued a near copy, but in reduced scale, of an American-made cowboy riding in a "Whoopee Car." The three-wheeled device has a specially

59

CLOCKWORK MOTORS

Animation was usually supplied by the power released from a tightly wound spiral steel spring, transmitted through a series of gear wheels, the speed being regulated by a governor. This mechanism, the clockwork motor, has powered the movements of tinplate toys for many years and is still used to operate modern-day mechanical toys. Simpler forms of this type of motor, usually found in the more cheaply produced toys, have a "piano wire" spring coiled along a simple cylinder made from tin, although this variation generally dropped from favour after World War II.

The firm of Jean Höfler of Fürth, Germany made a series of animal tin toys which featured the creatures perched on a kind of three-wheeled buggy. Pressing down the rear end of the buggy caused the animal to bend forwards and, at the same time, tensioned the spring in the mechanism. On release, the vehicle sped forwards, while the animal gradually resumed its upright position. This was a novel use of the clockwork motor, one which dispensed with the traditional method of winding the spring by using a key.

Another similar idea sometimes employed by toy vehicle manufacturers necessitated the vehicle being drawn backwards to tension the spring. Slight downward pressure on the toy caused a friction wheel to make contact with the running surface and revolve to wind up the motor. The German firm of Schuco featured this mode of propulsion in their famous "Studio" racing car of the 1930s, now being reproduced by the Germany company GAMA.

60

60
The appropriately named "Slugger Champions," made by the German firm of Biller in the 1950s, represents a boxing-ring with two tin fighters. The pugilists spar quite realistically, their arms flailing away at each other and sometimes hitting their target. The toy – the base is 3½in/9cm-square – is powered by a simple but quite ingenious clockwork mechanism. Similar toys were sold marked "Made in England."

CURIOSITIES

The "Whistling Tree" is a strange toy, quite rare in the United States and almost non-existent in Europe. This ghostly tree trunk has moving eyes and a loud whistling issues from its mouth. In addition, the stump moves around, pushing itself away from any obstacle which impedes its progress, and waves its arms up and down.

Another rare toy is the "Haunted House," a nicely lithographed tumbledown cottage which can, by operating a series of push buttons, be made to open the door to reveal a vampire figure, to show a black cat or a ghost at the window, and make a skeleton appear out of the chimney. The house also emits ghostly noises and the sound of whistling wind – quite a scary toy for a nervous child! A much tamer, although equally intriguing, clockwork version called "Animal House" features a variety of animals playing in and around a picturesque tree house.

61
This intriguing clockwork-powered "Animal House" novelty toy was made by Toplay of Japan in the 1950s. Attractively lithographed, it is 9in/23cm wide and features a bear and a monkey riding on a see-saw, a rabbit on a swing, and has different animal heads appearing at the window of the tree-house.

61

62

62
This unusual battery-operated butterfly was made by Alps Shoji of Japan in the 1950s. The wingspan is 6½in/17cm and, as the creature travels forward by remote-controlled battery power, the wings move realistically. The battery-holder is actually designed to represent a battery.

63
Made by Blomer & Schüler in the 1950s, this tinplate peacock is animated by clockwork so that it fans out its glorious tail feathers; 5in/13cm long.

TINPLATE ANIMALS

64
This well-produced example of a tin toy was made by Blomer & Schüler of Germany in the 1950s. The clockwork-powered turkey walks proudly along, fanning its tail as it goes, and is 6in/15cm long.

65
Little birds like this appeared in profusion, both in pre- and post-war years; the majority were attractively lithographed, although some were finished with a fabric covering. This one, by Nomura Toys of Japan, is 6½in/16cm long, although many smaller birds and some large ones were produced. Powered by clockwork, this bird pecks and chirps as it moves along.

63

64

65

designed clockwork mechanism which drives the vehicle alternately forwards and backwards in a jerking manner, giving the driver the appearance of riding a bucking bronco. Wells Brimtoy, in the 1950s, introduced a neat toy representing a milkman pulling along a contemporary electric-type milk truck. It displayed a sign, "Welsotoys Dairies," which was mechanically raised and lowered continuously during its journey. This little touch of extra movement is one which always adds to a toy's appeal to novelty enthusiasts.

One of the most famous of post-war novelties was the Arnold "Mac" motorcycle, which the rider actually mounts and dismounts as the ingenious mechanism allows it to start and stop. This toy was imitated later by the Japanese, who offered a much larger battery-powered version with similar action. Here is another toy which could also be included in the "automotive" class of collectible toys. See the chapter on Tin Toy Motor Vehicles for more details of this and other "cross-over" toys.

BATTERY TOYS

Without a shadow of doubt, Japan was the king of battery-toy producers. Although Germany had introduced a few battery-operated toys – Schuco, in particular – that country mainly concentrated its efforts in the realm of model road

66

These are just some of the battery-operated and clockwork toys produced by Nomura Toys of Tokyo, Japan in the 1950s, and illustrated in a contemporary trade catalog issued by the company.

67

Made by Nomura Toys, Tokyo, and probably the best-known post-war Japanese battery toy of all, "Charlie Weaver" obviously enjoys the strong liquor he appears to pour out of his flask and swallow. The drink causes strange effects, however – his face turns red and smoke pours out of his ears! Like most of Japan's products, the rich United States market was their main target – and Charlie was, in those days, a well-known American TV character. The toy is 12½in/32cm tall.

68

The Japanese occasionally produced smaller-scale, clockwork versions of their popular battery figures. This is a 7in/18cm-tall version of "The Bartender," itself a variation on the "Charlie Weaver" battery toy. His clockwork mechanism makes him appear to pour himself a drink from a cocktail shaker, but he is unable to turn red in the face and emit smoke from his ears like his battery-powered big brother! Both versions were made by Nomura Toys of Japan in the 1950s.

vehicles and aircraft. Among all the battery-operated cars, trains, aircraft, and space toys it was the Japanese who came nearest to recreating the art of the automata-makers of old. Not on such a complex and expensive scale, it is true; but they produced toys to a fairly high standard for the relatively low prices at which they were marketed. Their humanoid figures were perhaps the most amazing and practically everyone who is interested in toys at all has come across "Charlie Weaver."

Like the majority of Japan's toy production, "Charlie" was aimed at the rich American market, although the toys also reached other countries. Only Americans were to know that a Charlie Weaver actually existed and that the boozy hillbilly was based on a character created by vaudeville star Cliff Arquette. He became widely known through his appearance as Charlie Weaver on American radio and TV in the 1940s. Any enthusiast who would like to see Arquette's Charlie Weaver in action should watch out for the Abbot and Costello movie, *She'll Be Coming Round the Mountain,* appearing on TV, in which he makes an appearance with the comedians. The toy features Charlie behind a

68

69

bar, shaking a cocktail which he then goes through the motion of drinking; his face then turns red (internal lighting glowing through his vinyl features) and smoke issues from his ears! Though this must surely be among the commonest of all battery toys, Charlie Weaver is nevertheless a clever example of Japanese engineering ingenuity.

The same toy was also issued, with a different head and a change of lithography, as "The Bartender." Other figural toys include an "Indian Joe" playing drums; "Gino the Balloon Man," who actually inflates small balloons from a "gas cylinder;" a "Hula Hoop Girl;" "Smoking Grandpa," who rocks himself in a chair while smoking a glowing pipe; "McGregor," the seated cigar-smoking Scot who can stand up and sit down; and "Miss Friday, the Typist," who clatters away on her typewriter.

69

This remote-controlled battery toy was named "The Happy Miner" by its maker, Ashai of Japan. The gnome-like figure can walk forwards, pushing his wheelbarrow, and his eyes light up. He is 11½in/29cm tall and dates from the 1960s.

70

70
This "Strutting Sam" is a 1950s Japanese battery-operated version of similar dancing-man toys produced in pre-war days both in Germany and the United States. The Japanese issued other similar toys with clockwork mechanisms around the same period. This example is 10½in/27cm tall.

71
This "Tric-Cycling Clown" pedals along on a battery-powered uni-cycle, balancing an illuminated ball in each hand at the same time. This toy was produced by MT Toys of Japan in the 1960s, and is 10in/25cm high.

The Cragstan "Crapshooter" gambles by throwing dice he shakes first in a cup. He holds dollar bills in the hand, and chews gum – or tobacco? – in anticipation of a win. Everyone likes "Good Time Charlie," the battery toy which represents a top-hatted drunk enjoying a quick nip from his flask while seated on a dustbin by a street lamp. Like "Charlie Weaver," his face turns red after each swig at the bottle! "Chef Cook" works over an illuminated stove, busily making – and tossing – a pancake, at the same time seasoning it from a shaker in his left hand. This toy has also been produced with a vinyl pig's head and retitled "Piggy Cook." There are virtually hundreds of these toys – an ideal field for collecting, although some of them are much harder to find than others. But that only makes the game more interesting.

71

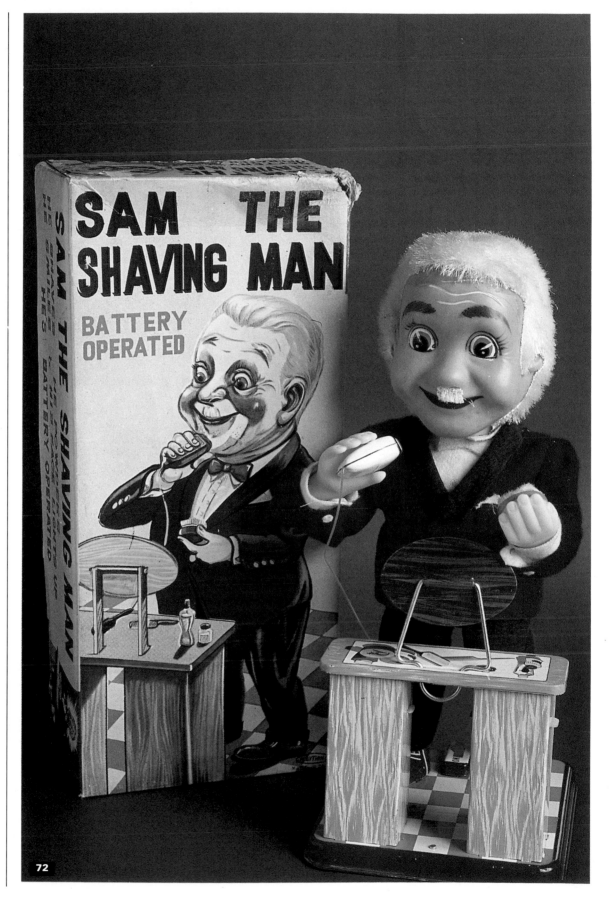

72

"Sam the Shaving Man" is one of the rarer Japanese battery-operated novelty figures which appeared on the market in the 1950s. He is 12½in/32cm tall and his actions include shaving with an electric razor, powdering his face (imitation talcum dust rising from his powder puff), and his face lights up when he admires the results in the mirror. The toy is marked "Plaything Made in Japan," but the actual maker is unknown.

73

74

"Smokey Bear," an animated battery toy from Marusan Toys of Japan, is controlled from a remote-wired battery holder. He will walk forwards, taking puffs from his pipe which actually lights up and emits smoke. At 8in/20cm in height, he is one of the smaller battery toys produced in the 1950s.

74

75

73
The "Circus Lion" offers you the chance to become a lion-tamer without danger! Stand the lion on the special mat (containing the hidden levers which operate the battery-powered mechanism beneath the toy) and command it to "sit up," at the same striking one side of the mat with the special "lion-tamer's stick" provided. If you have hit the correct hidden lever, the lion rears up, pawing the air and growling. Command him to sit, hitting the other side of the mat, and the lion stops growling and pawing and sits down. This great toy from Rock Valley Toys of Japan was produced in the 1950s and is around 12in/30cm tall.

75
"Peppermint Twist" is a late 1960s animated plastic doll mounted on a tinplate base, which contains its battery-operated mechanism and the batteries. This hard-to-find toy is constructed mainly in plastic so that the figure can imitate the gyrating movements of the "twist" dance that it commemorates so admirably. The toy is 12½in/32cm tall and was manufactured by the Mego Corporation of Japan.

The animal figures came in an equally wide — if not wider — range than did their human counterparts. These include battery-operated bears playing accordions; cymbal-clashing monkeys; a "Hungry Cat" whose eyes mischievously light up while it tries to catch goldfish in a bowl; a "Popcorn Vendor Duck" pushing a cart with a receptacle full of popping corn; a vacuum-cleaning lady rabbit; and the doggie "Burger Chef," another variation on the "Chef Cook" toy. Other Japanese triumphs include the "Musical Bulldog," which smokes a "lighted" cigar while he "plays" the piano; a "Hungry Baby Bear," which depicts Mummy Bear feeding her young one from a bottle. The "Playful Dog" is amused by a wriggling caterpillar; and a "Popcorn Vendor Bear" rides a three-wheeler and sells "freshly" popping corn.

It is interesting to note that a few of the Japanese battery toys were also manufactured in much smaller scale and operated by clockwork motors.

76
This battery-operated "Accordion Clown," produced by Rock Valley Toys of Japan in the 1950s, is ingeniously constructed and hard-to-find. The toy is 12in/30cm tall and the clown is accompanied by the little cymbal-clashing monkey.

76

Character Toys

When toys are manufactured in the form of well-known characters which have achieved their popularity on the cinema or television screen, or through comic-strip cartoons, they are referred to as "character toys" by toy enthusiasts. Because of their generally interesting appearance and the fact that they are usually capable of presenting amusing mechanical actions, these character toys may also be classed as members of the large family of novelty figure toys. The fans of the original characters these playthings represent are the greatest admirers of toys falling under this particular classification. They provide plenty of competition for members of the general novelty-toy collecting fraternity in their common search for suitable examples to add to their personal collections. This double demand obviously tends to push up the market value of such toys.

The interest in these particular playthings extends way back into the pre-war days of tinplate toys, with animated figures from the Walt Disney cartoon movies being among the most highly appreciated examples. The revival of the international tinplate toy industry following World War II saw quite a variety of new character toys appearing on the market once again. Mickey Mouse, Donald Duck, and company were well represented, as was Popeye. Such cartoon notabilities as Tom & Jerry, Mr Magoo, The Flintstones, and Topo Gigio have also been commemorated, to a lesser degree, during the same period.

77

77
The clockwork "Mickey Mouse Xylophone" is a rare toy from the 1950s made by Linemar Toys of Japan. Mickey "plink-plonks" on the tin xylophone but no actual tune is emitted. This toy, much sought after by collectors of cartoon character toys, is 6in/15 cm high.

78

No one can fail to recognize Donald Duck, the world-famous Walt Disney character. The 6in/15cm-tall clockwork figure depicted here is tinplate, with plastic bill and feet. This toy was introduced by the German firm, Schuco, in the 1950s, although another Donald Duck was also issued by the company in pre-war days.

79

A 1970s Japanese tinplate battery toy, this "Mickey Mouse & Donald Duck Fire Engine" is 16½in/42cm long and features "mystery action," flashing red light, ringing bell sound, and the Donald Duck sways from side to side. The figures and the base of the toy are all made of plastic. This colorful toy, made by Masudaya, has special appeal to Disney-character collectors.

DISNEY CHARACTERS

Mickey Mouse and his Disney friends appeared in toy form in many of the battery, friction, and clockwork toys exported worldwide by Japan. Schuco, of Germany, reissued a modified example of their pre-war Donald Duck while Wells-Brimtoy in the UK introduced a new version of their pre-war "Mickey Mouse Handcar" boxed railway-set. One popular, colorful toy which appeared in the 1950s was a fine tinplate "Goofy the Gardener," made by Marx at their UK factory. An obviously cheerful Goofy pushes his barrow along, activated by a clockwork motor built into the truck.

Desirable Mickey Mouse toys from Japan include a clockwork all-tin toy of Mickey playing a xylophone and a remote-controlled battery-toy of Mickey, with illuminated eyes, walking along and playing a drum. One highly sought-after Mickey Mouse battery toy depicts this popular character as "Mickey the Magician." Here the famous mouse waves his magic wand and mysteriously causes a chicken to alternately appear and disappear from beneath a top hat! This is a particularly ingenious toy, based on the actions of complicated automata of earlier years.

79

OTHER CARTOON FIGURES

Popeye's popularity is undoubted and a new series of his cartoons has been drawn for TV transmission – although his followers generally agree that the original animated cartoons were far superior. Among all the tinplate Popeye toys perhaps the "Bubble Blowing Popeye" and the "Smoking Popeye" are the most ingenious. In the former, Popeye holds a can of his favorite food, spinach, in one hand and an illuminated pipe in the other. Both arms move up and down as he blows a series of bubbles from his mouth! In the latter example Popeye is again featured smoking a lit pipe, but is seated on a disproportionately large can of spinach; he turns his head and exhales smoke while waving his right arm. These toys are both of Japanese origin, as is the popular clockwork figural tin toy featuring a roller-skating Popeye.

"Fred Flintstone on Dino" and "Fred Flintstone's Bedrock Band" are amusingly intriguing toys evocative of the well-known TV cartoon series. The "Fred Flintstone Car," a tinplate vehicle of prehistoric appearance with a plastic Fred at the driving wheel, is also worth looking out for. Toys of this period generally introduced a certain amount of plastic material into their make-up, and this was especially so with cartoon figures. Molded vinyl heads actually led to superior likenesses to the faces of the characters they represented and were obviously more economical to produce than their machine-pressed tinplate predecessors. The crotchety shortsighted Mr Magoo appeared as the driver of a typical 1950s–1960s battery-operated "old-time" styled motor car. His head, fashioned from vinyl, was a very good likeness and the whole represents an excellent example of a cartoon character toy.

Another once internationally-famous character was the Italian mouse-puppet Topo Gigio which became famous for a while on TV in many countries, resulting in an amusing Japanese battery toy being produced in his memory. Topo Gigio is actually molded from vinyl, but he is featured playing a tinplate xylophone;

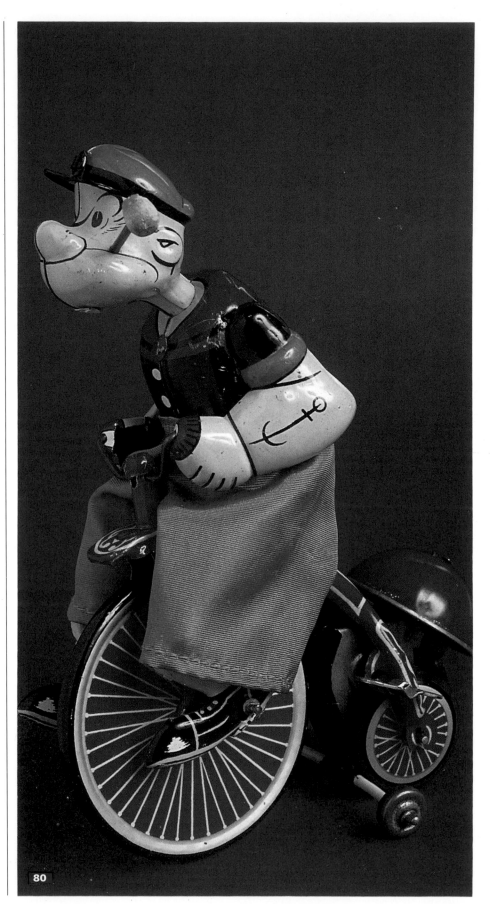

80

80 **81**

Here are two much sought-after Popeye character toys made by Linemar of Japan in the 1950s. The first example is the 6in/15cm-high, clockwork "Popeye on Tricycle." The second example is the clockwork "Popeye Skater," a well-produced toy, 6½in/ 16cm tall, representing Popeye skating along while holding up a can of his famous spinach.

81

the mechanism is programmed to allow him to accurately pick out the notes of "London Bridge is Falling Down." This toy was also marketed with the American cartoon character Dennis the Menace in place of Topo Gigio. (Not to be confused with the British comic character of the same name; the American Dennis the Menace is known simply as "Dennis" in the UK, to avoid confusion.) The toy was also issued with the Disney-character Pinocchio playing the instrument.

FILM AND COMIC-STRIP CHARACTERS

The James Bond movies were received with international acclaim and the Japanese were quick to introduce ingenious battery-operated replicas of 007's famous gadget-riddled car. Even the ejection seat could be triggered off to throw the passenger through the open sun roof! While some of these cars were openly sold carrying the name "James Bond" and the car had the registration plate "007," others exist bearing such names as "Secret Agent Car" and an alternative registration number – obviously in an attempt to avoid payment of copyright charges! Today such toys are no

82

This Japanese-produced James Bond-style Aston-Martin is fitted with all the "007" gagetry, including the famous ejector-seat for undesirable passengers – but no 007 registration plate. The lack of such specific James Bond references on the car or its box suggests that the toy is unofficial – an attempt by the makers to avoid paying copyright dues. Dating to the 1960s, the car is 8½in/22cm long.

longer made in tinplate, though recently a series of "Batman" and "Joker" clockwork tin toys have been manufactured in the Far East to appease the collectors' market – also fired no doubt by the launch of the popular *Batman* movie starring Jack Nicholson as the Joker.

In the 1950s two walking Batman figural toys were marketed; one was slightly smaller than the other and had an illuminated "Batman" insignia on its chest. These are now very desirable and highly-priced toys, each being something of a rarity. Batman interest is certainly thriving and most of the commemorative Batman tin toys are eagerly snapped up at toy collectors' fairs and auction sales. Superman is another popular fantasy hero and he is remembered in an ingeniously made Japanese battery toy which was marketed during the early post-war years. It is designed to re-enact an episode in which the articulated tinplate Superman uses his tremendous powers in grappling with an army tank. A masterpiece of toy technology, this item depicts Superman gradually overcoming his enemy by pushing the tank backwards and eventually hoisting its front completely off the ground.

Other Japanese-produced tinplate figures based on movie, TV, and mythical characters include the "Abominable Snowman," "Godzilla," "King Kong," "Frankenstein's Monster," and "Alley the Alligator." All battery-operated, they date from the 1950s and '60s.

Pop musicians were not forgotten either, and a Japanese-made friction-operated tin car featuring The Monkees

84

85
This fascinating 10in/ 26cm-tall tinplate battery toy represents "Godzilla," the walking fire-breathing monster from Japanese mythology and films – much popularized in American B-feature movies. It was produced by Bullmark of Tokyo in the 1960s.

83
This novelty toy, is a 5in/ 13cm-tall furry clockwork "Yeti" that ambles along when wound up. Made in Japan in the 1950s, the manufacturer is unknown.

83

This classic battery-operated character toy features Superman battling with a tank. The super-hero finally disables the tank by lifting the front end high off the ground. Made by Linemar of Japan in the early post-war years, it is 8½in/ 21cm in length.

delighted the group's fans when it appeared in the 1960s. The figures of the pop group riding in the car were made from plastic. An added novelty was an internal battery-operated recorder which would reproduce the sound of the group rendering their signature tune "We Are the Monkees!"

FATHER CHRISTMAS TOYS

Another highly collectible character who does not have to depend upon magazines, movies, or television to maintain his popularity is dear old Santa Claus. Tin toys in his form — or any other form, it would seem — now enjoy widespread popularity. Santa first became collectible in the United States, where the majority of media-based characters were created and where the hobby of collecting their commemoratives thrives. Collecting Santa Claus, or Father Christmas if you prefer, is closely allied to the hobby of accumulating Christmas ephemera of all kinds — again, an interest which has a large following in the United States in particular.

Father Christmas has appeared in tin-plate form for a number of years, many examples appearing from Germany in the post-war period, with Arnold being responsible for a small, neatly produced clockwork model. A similar, but simpler clockwork figure was marketed by the British firm of Wells-Brimtoy in the early 1950s; this had a rocking motion which

propelled it along. The same pressing was economically redecorated to sell as a clown!

Obviously the Japanese could not afford to ignore Father Christmas in their output of playthings and he figures largely in their range of toy products. Their Santa Claus toys are both clockwork and battery-powered — mainly the latter. The old gentleman was featured ringing a handbell, riding various vehicles, and sitting upon the roof of a house with a pile of packages, ready to make a delivery! This last toy also served as a money bank and, when a coin is dropped through the slot, Santa's eyes light up, his head moves, and he rings his handbell. Another such battery toy, which also doubles as a mechanical bank, has a Father Christmas who pretends to answer the telephone when dialled on an extension phone, after dropping a coin through the slot.

Specializing in the collecting of character toys can lead to a very rewarding hobby and a group of such items will certainly make for a colorful and amusing showcase display. The international popularity of this particular theme leads to much market competition, however, and, generally-speaking, it is a sellers' market.

Some character toys, such as the famous 1950s Japanese battery-operated "Charlie Weaver" figure, are mentioned in detail elsewhere in this book — see the chapter on Tinplate Figures for some more examples.

The American ventriloquist Edgar Bergen's famous dummy, Charlie MacCarthy, is remembered in this character toy from Marx of the United States. He drives a bucking clockwork jeep and the toy was made in the 1940s to '50s.

Tin Toy Motor Vehicles

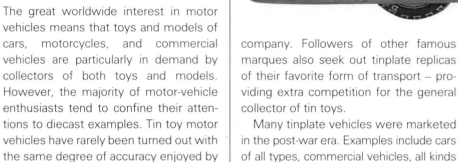

87
This toy car, of no particular make, was produced by the British firm of Chad Valley in the early post-war years and is 9in/23cm long. Such toys were aimed at the cheaper end of the trade, but were well made and designed and are now popular collectibles.

The great worldwide interest in motor vehicles means that toys and models of cars, motorcycles, and commercial vehicles are particularly in demand by collectors of both toys and models. However, the majority of motor-vehicle enthusiasts tend to confine their attentions to diecast examples. Tin toy motor vehicles have rarely been turned out with the same degree of accuracy enjoyed by their diecast counterparts. Even so, tinplate examples are always highly sought-after – and usually carry relatively high prices accordingly.

company. Followers of other famous marques also seek out tinplate replicas of their favorite form of transport – providing extra competition for the general collector of tin toys.

Many tinplate vehicles were marketed in the post-war era. Examples include cars of all types, commercial vehicles, all kinds of public transport, and motorcycles. Unlike their diecast counterparts, standardization of scale hardly exists and models come in all sizes.

88
This 9in/23cm-long clockwork-driven car is a model of a Mercedes 220S, named "Magic Optomat" by its German toymaker, Hubert Kienberger – it carries the company's "Huki" trademark. Made in the 1950s to '60s, the car was designed to turn away from the edge of a table, so preventing a tumble, and the heads of the driver and passenger move as the car travels along.

87

Many of the road vehicles produced as toys often represent no particular make of car or truck, but there are those which do. These often attract the attention of collectors who specialize in the products of particular road-vehicle manufacturers. A Rolls-Royce fanatic will, for instance, be interested in acquiring models and toys based on the products of that car

FROM TRUCKS TO LIMOUSINES

Motor Vehicles from Japan
Highly sought-after internationally are the wonderful early post-war American-style toy limousines produced in Japan from around the 1950s. These flashy, bulbous, chrome-plated model cars cap-

90
This interesting small clockwork car, produced in the 1950s by the French manufacturer, Joustra, is 5in/13cm long. When the mechanism is wound up to set the car running, it performs a perfect "Y-"turn.

90

ture perfectly the nostalgic atmosphere of the period. Japanese toy designers produced these American limousines as skillful mimics of the original machines, although they are not strictly accurate miniature replicas by any means. These were simply marvelous toys, often fitted with novelty actions, including the "bump-and-go" mechanism and electric lighting. Some had the luxury of four-speed gears and working horns; even, in some cases, key ignition. They are well worth looking out for, but they do not generally come cheaply.

The best of these models came from Bandai of Tokyo, one of Japan's leading toy manufacturers. A particularly fine example is the firm's excellent model of a 1957 Ford Fairplane. Other Japanese

89

89
A novelty car from Joustra, this 1950s clockwork toy runs along, then stops, the door opening to reveal the tinplate driver alighting to see that the car's hood has sprung open. This 5in/13cm-long car represents an interesting attempt by the French to make novelty toys in the German style.

MONEY-BOX CARS

91 **92**

Here are two examples of Japanese-made toy cars doubling as mobile savings banks. The first example, produced by Daiya in the 1970s, is a 6½in/16cm-long battery-operated car. However, it refuses to move until a coin is dropped through a slot in the top of the vehicle. The second example is a friction-drive armored car, measuring 10in/25cm, made by Horikawa in the 1950s. It has locking rear doors which can be unlocked with the key provided; as the doors slowly swing open, a warning alarm bell sounds.

91

92

93

The "Auto Obstacle" was one of a small series of mechanical novelty tinplate cars brought out by Joustra of France in the 1950s. It is cleverly designed not to run off the edge of a table, and also to turn away from obstacles (hence its name). To perform this latter feat, it is uniquely fitted with a laterally revolving wheel which is powered by the clockwork mechanism that lies partially hidden beneath its streamlined hood. The car is 5½in/14cm in length.

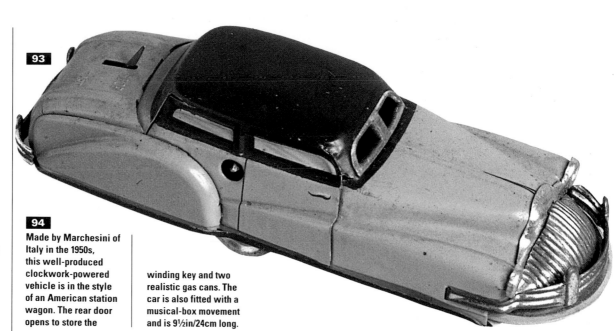

93

94

Made by Marchesini of Italy in the 1950s, this well-produced clockwork-powered vehicle is in the style of an American station wagon. The rear door opens to store the winding key and two realistic gas cans. The car is also fitted with a musical-box movement and is 9½in/24cm long.

94

companies, such as Haji, Asahi and Nomura, contributed similar fine examples of contemporary cars. A 1964 catalogue issued by the Nomura Toy Company shows their selection of tinplate automobiles to include comparatively few battery-operated cars. Their model Buick and Chevrolet saloons used friction drive, as did their Police Patrol Car, Fire Chief Car, and the Ambulance Car, which were all based on their Buick model. The only battery-operated model automobiles offered were a Sports Car and a Mystery-Action Benz, along with a remote-control version of the Benz.

Nomura's battery-operated Army Jeep and Police Jeep lean towards the novelty toy description, with their tinplate passengers going through the actions of answering a mobile telephone. Their catalog details a series of novelty battery-operated automotive toys including a Police Car, a "Smokey Bear" driving a Jeep, a "Fire Chief Car," an "Old-Fashioned Fire Engine," a "Hot-Rod," an "Old Fashioned Car," a "Grand-Pa Car,"

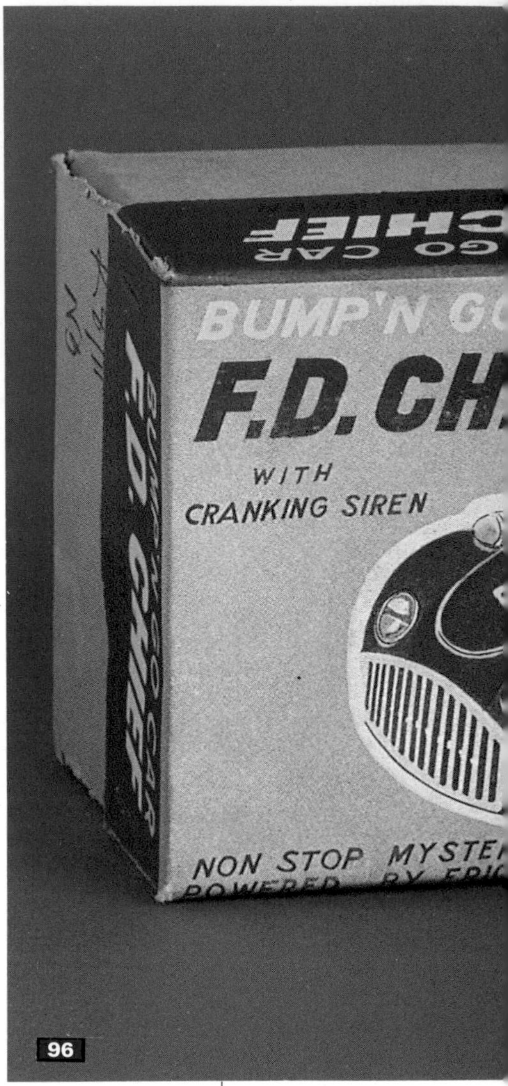

96
Another Japanese product styled for the American market, this 10½in/27cm-long "Fire Department Fire Chief" toy is powered by friction-drive and dates from the 1950s to '60s. The driver's head is "pre-plastic" and formed from tinplate. As the car journeys along, the driver winds the handle of the warning siren to clear the road. Its "mystery action" makes the vehicle by-pass any obstacles that might impede its progress.

96

95
This American-style "Highway Patrol Car" is by Daiya of Japan. Battery-operated, and 10½in/27cm in length, the uniformed driver moves his arm to fire his flashing gun. The well-made toy has the usual "mystery action" and dates from the 1970s.

95

97
This fine 14in/35cm-long tinplate battery-operated Mercedes saloon was produced by Ichiko Kogyo of Japan in the 1960s.

98

99

98

This car appeared in the 1950s from Nomura Toys of Japan and was named "Hot Rod." Battery-operated, it has "bump-and-go" action and an illuminated engine. The driver's head also turns from side to side. A very neatly made, good-quality toy, it is 7in/18cm in length.

99

Another battery-operated "old-time" car, this example by Nomura Toys of Japan is rather unusual. It is known as "Willie the Walking Car" since, as well as running normally on its wheels, it can also walk; the wheels act as legs and the car ambles along like a rather inelegant quadruped. The face on its radiator lights up and its headlights move up and down like blinking eyes. A true novelty toy, made in the late 1960s, it is controlled remotely from a hand-held battery case, and is 10in/25cm long.

100

100
The increased amount of plastic incorporated in this tinplate vehicle dates it from the 1970s. It is similar in action to many of the earlier battery-operated "old-time" novelty cars which issued from Japan in abundance following World War II. Among its many actions, this car lights up to reveal the silhouettes of its passengers on the opaque windows; it is 9½in/24cm long.

and an "Antique Car." The latter, when switched on, runs along, stops and shakes violently, while its driver struggles to re-gain control and smoke issues from the radiator! This was one of the most popular toys of its day.

Examples from Germany
In Germany, the old-established firm of Schreyer & Co, better known by its "Schuco" trademark, produced a number of motor vehicles, ranging from American limousines to a fascinating battery-powered fire engine. In pre-war years the company had made a variety of in-genious little tin toy cars, some of which were reintroduced after the war. A parti-cularly good seller for Schuco in the 1930s was their "Studio" Mercedes racing car, which came complete with a jack and spanners for removing the hubs to change the wheels, and a lever to remove the tires from the wheels. The "Studio" was

also steerable and its clockwork mechan-ism could either be wound by a crank-shaped key, or by depressing the car and pulling it backwards a short distance. This model was marketed once again after the war, along with some of the firm's other novelty cars. One of them, the "Command Car," could be stopped and started by blowing a special whistle. This directed a blast of air through the grille in the car roof, switching the clockwork mechanism on and off.

In the 1960s Schuco introduced their "Oldtimer" series, which included clock-work models of a 1902 Mercedes Simplex and a 1911 Renault 6CV Voiturette, a 1909 Opel Doktor-Wagen, and a Mercer Racing Car. Each of these models could run in neutral, their engines "ticking over" with the bodywork shaking realistically. The Opel had a refined mechanism which allowed the hood to be raised mechanic-ally, while the Mercedes had the most complicated mechanism of the series, designed to allow the fully-wound motor to be started by winding the crank handle – and, like the real car, it did not always fire first time! An ingenious design feature – or an amusing coincidence? Their Model "T" Ford, containing a musical movement, was only marketed for a short spell. The last car to be added to the series was the Renault, which featured an engine with visible sparking plugs, and worked from a small battery. This is the rarest of the series, produced only for a short period.

The "Oldtimer" cars first appeared with cast-metal wheels; later they were molded from plastic. Severe cost cutting, in the course of time, resulted in a general cheapening of the models. The Mercedes lost its crank-handle start, the Mercer lost its steering-wheel-mounted mini-windscreen, and similar refinements on all the models disappeared. To make matters worse, the vehicles were finished in the most appalling color schemes. It was a sad signal of the approaching decline which was to ultimately affect all tin toy manufacturers worldwide.

Some Schuco toys were actually manufactured for the company under licence by the old-established German firm of Georg Mangold, trading as GAMA. One particularly notable novelty product made by Mangold for Schuco in the 1950s was the "Fex," a tinplate toy car designed to roll over when taking a bend at speed. In a clever conservation of power, the clockwork mechanism cut out as the car turned over. Once the vehicle had its wheels back on the ground, the motor switched on again. The action repeated until the power ran out – which did not take very long. However, the stress suffered by the quick-release spring is obvious by the number of surviving examples which have been left with inoperative mechanisms. Also, the relatively fragile diecast front bumpers are often

101

This fire engine and trailer was sold by GAMA, Germany, in the 1950s and is marked "US Zone of Germany." It has friction-drive, emits a siren sound, and the trailer can actually pump water through the hosepipe. It is 12in/31cm in total length.

102

This ingenious toy car, known as the "Cabrio 359," came from the German firm of Kellermann in the 1950s. It has a clockwork motor and, by the flick of a switch under its chassis, can be swiftly transformed from a saloon car to an open tourer, complete with driver.

101

102

103
This 4½in/11cm-long VW "Beetle," decorated in the livery of the German Post Office, is one of the later models in the "Rollo Series," produced by Kellermann

of Germany in the 1950s to '60s. The firm produced a splendid range of friction-drive scale model cars in this series, ranging from a fire engine to a motor coach; the metal pressing in all the various models was of the finest quality.

103

104

FORWARD-FRICTION MECHANISMS

This method of propulsion has been used to power toys as far back as the turn of the century. The simplest form consists of a heavy flywheel which is set spinning, gyroscope fashion, by pulling hard on a coiled string wound around a pulley fixed to the flywheel's axle. Once set spinning at a high revolution rate, sufficient power is generated to start a simple toy moving for a reasonable length of time.

A more developed version of this type of mechanism gears the heavy flywheel to the toy vehicle's rear wheels; when the owner causes the rear wheel to spin rapidly in the right direction the impetus of the spinning flywheel propels the toy forward when released.

104

Small 5in/13cm-long tinplate saloon cars like this, powered by tiny electric motors, appeared on the market in the 1950s to 1960s, apparently as a prelude to the well-produced "Rollo Series," which were similar-scale models fitted with friction-drive mechanisms. They were manufactured by the old-established German company of Kellermann.

105

This friction-drive 9in/23cm-long Citroën car dates from the 1960s. It is an unusual example of a toy manufactured by the German firm of Tipp & Co – once owned by Philipp Ullman – for the British firm of Mettoy, founded by Ullman after he fled the Nazi regime in the late 1930s.

105

broken off, through hitting walls at speed. GAMA are now reintroducing several Schuco toys, using the original machinery (see the feature on Present-Day Reissues of Post-War Tin Toys).

S Günthermann, one of Germany's leading toy producers, introduced a pleasing range of motor vehicles in the post-war years. In particular, the company was responsible for a nice series of Mercedes vans in differing guises, the selection ranging from mini-buses to military vehicles. Their contemporary cars appeared as open-topped tourers, station wagons, and ambulances; some with electric and others with clockwork motors. Günthermann's Ford Compact Auto was battery powered by a remote-control cable which also operated the car's steering.

In the 1960s and '70s, the old-established firm of Kellermann of Nuremberg introduced a number of excellent, accurately designed model vehicles which could, at first glance, be taken for diecast models. They were made to the same scale, but the bodies were of tinplate pressed into perfect shape, without any trace of a wrinkle. The immaculately turned-out models included examples of cars such as the VW Beetle, the Mercedes 280 SE, and the Ford Capri. The company also produced an excellent model house trailer, which could be towed behind any of the cars, as well as a fine fire engine and a Mercedes cement-mixer. All the models had friction-drive mechanisms. These items are not often seen at toy fairs — and, when they do turn up, are curiously neglected by collectors. First introduced in 1954, and known as the "Rollo Series," they are definitely worth looking out for and should promise reasonable investment potential. One or two earlier examples were furnished with tiny electric motors providing the power. The scale and bodywork were similar to the "Rollo Series," but they were not quite as perfectly pressed as their friction-driven counterparts.

The German firm of Tipp & Co produced many fine tin toys prior to World War II. Its owner Phillipp Ullman fled to England from the Nazi regime in 1933 and the company fell into the hands of the German government. The original Tipp & Co survived the ravages of war and began issuing tin toys once again. They marketed a selection of well-produced and well-finished cars, trucks, and fire engines. One basic truck chassis, with friction-drive mechanism, was turned out as a flat-backed truck, a canvas-covered truck, a breakdown truck, a side-tipper, and an "Express" delivery truck. The company's fine model of a VW van appeared in various guises, too, including a police van, a fire service truck, a flat-backed van, a mail van, and a canvas-covered "Express" delivery truck. Their large "Mercedes Monopisto" racing car with friction drive — and a siren for sound effect — was especially attractive.

MYSTERY ACTION

One mechanical contrivance which is found in many automated tin toys is the "mystery action," also known as "push-and-go" or "bump-and-go" action. This is an ingeniously designed arrangement which allows the axle of the two front wheels of a toy vehicle to revolve laterally. The wheels carry the toy forward in a straight line but, when progress is impeded, the wheel axle turns to guide the vehicle away from the object that lies in its path.

The "mystery action" is found in a few clockwork-powered toys, but exists mainly in the many battery novelty toys produced by Japanese manufacturers. Such toy cars — or wheeled boats or railway engines, for that matter — can slowly work their way out of the tightest corner by steadily pushing away from the walls until they eventually escape, or the batteries become exhausted!

British products

Phillipp Ullman's new firm, Mettoy, based in England, also marketed many interesting tin road-vehicles after the war, among which were two large clockwork limousines, one a Rolls-Royce, the other a vehicle of no particular make. The bodies of both cars were virtually identical, except the Rolls lacked a sliding roof, and the other limo didn't have a Rolls radiator. The firm's range of toys included several cars and trucks — even racing cars and camouflaged military vehicles.

Two particularly colorful items were the "OK Biscuits" and the "Bingo's Circus" clockwork trucks — the same toy turned out with different artwork. Another unusual Mettoy vehicle was a six-wheel truck designed to transport the detachable airplane with which it was sold. The plane itself was a standard Mettoy product of a type marketed separately, fitted with a clockwork mechanism.

Several car trailers were also produced by the firm, again using the same pressing but finished in various formats. The most curious of these was a wartime mobile canteen printed with a long window through which the volunteer lady helpers are seen serving behind an array of tea urns and cakes. Another curiosity is an oil tanker displaying the word "Pool." This did not denote a brand of gasoline, as would be expected today, but referred to the mixture of fuel "pooled" from various sources. Brand names disappeared for the duration of the war. Both of these examples were still available for a short period after the war.

A range of small-scale road vehicles called Minics were manufactured in the UK by the firm of Lines Brothers, trading under the name of Tri-ang. These small cars, trucks, and buses, were marketed in the pre-war years, and reappeared again after the war. Well made and attractive,

106
A popular, and fairly rare, tinplate toy, this "OK Biscuits" van was produced by the British firm of Mettoy in the late 1950s. It has a clockwork mechanism that powers its movement and is 9½in/24cm long.

107
These three small vans, just 3in/8cm each in length, were produced by Wells-Brimtoy, a British toymaker, in the late 1950s to '60s. They are clockwork-powered and, although they are mainly formed from tinplate, their cabs are molded from plastic. They represent, from left to right, a mobile refreshment van, a Royal Mail van and an ambulance.

106

107

these tinplate toys were originally issued with clockwork mechanisms and, later, friction drives. Finally, as the company ran into the difficulties that seriously affected toy producers in general, Minics were given plastic bodies. In general, Minics were neglected as popular collectibles until quite recently – the lack of interest probably due to the fact that die-cast collectors shunned tinplate models and tinplate collectors thought them too small. Only the buses in the range appeared to have any particular value,

108

Examples of this fine clockwork tinplate farm tractor are not very hard to find, even though they were produced in the 1950s. They were made by Mettoy, UK, who also issued various agricultural implements as add-ons, both separately and as a boxed set.

108

109

110

111

111
This is a 1950s Tri-ang Minic model of a cleansing department garbage truck. It is clockwork-powered and 5in/13cm long.

112
This 1950s Minic traction engine with trailer is 9in/22cm in total length. The clockwork-powered traction engine is tinplate with plastic wheels; earlier models were fitted with wooden wheels.

109
This is a rare and highly desirable Tri-ang "Minic" boxed set dating from the 1950s, containing clockwork-powered "mechanical horses" and a variety of trailers. The British firm of Lines Bros, trading under the name Tri-ang, first introduced Minic toys just before World War II. The earlier examples were all clockwork-powered, although friction-drive was introduced later, and towards the end of their reign plastic bodies began to replace tinplate.

110
This 1950s Minic breakdown truck, 7in/18cm in length, comes with two clockwork mechanisms – one to drive the vehicle, the other to power the crane.

112

113
This 1950s clockwork Minic model depicts a small 9in/23cm-long boat transporter. The vehicle is tinplate; the boat is plastic and fitted with a clockwork motor so it can be sailed in the bath.

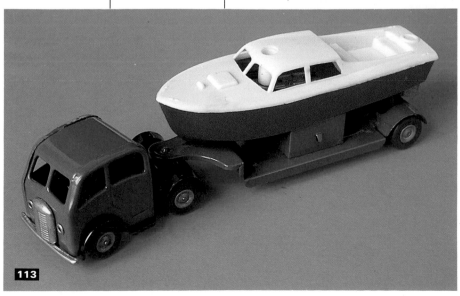

113

114

114
The Buddy L toy
company of the United
States produced this
large-scale metal pick-
up truck in the 1960s.

with their special appeal to model-bus collectors. Suddenly, the situation changed: Minic collecting became fashionable and examples are now highly sought-after by collectors and traders alike, greatly affecting their value.

Steel Plate Motor Vehicles
In the United States big-scale metal toys made from steel plate have always been popular, but are not generally so collectible in Europe. Strictly speaking, such toys do not fall within the tinplate classification, but they are worth a mention, nevertheless. Tonka have been prolific producers of such automotive toys since World War II. In the UK, Lines Brothers had marketed a range of large sheet-metal toys in the 1930s, under their Tri-ang label, and reintroduced them in the 1950s. The early post-war Tri-ang models featured a Transport Van with rubber-tired wheels. Its attraction, especially to today's collectors, is the display of nostalgic posters on the sides of the vehicle. Other Tri-ang models of the era included a milk truck with metal churns, a "Shell" petrol tanker, a brick truck with multi-colored

bricks, a fire truck with ringing bell, and a construction truck. These large steel toys were designed to be pulled, or pushed along in play – the construction truck actually came equipped with a remote steering wheel at the end of a rod. The young owner could walk behind, pushing and guiding the vehicle via the rod, which steered the front wheels through a universal joint coupling.

As recently as the 1970s the Tri-ang catalogs were illustrating their "Hi-Way" selection of Freightliner trucks – a rescue service vehicle, tipper truck, milk truck with plastic milk bottles, fire tender, and brick truck. The catalogs also offered a variety of smaller commercial vehicles in the "Mini Hi-Way" range. These generally had plastic accessories around a pressed-steel body. Other models, such as the racing car and military series, introduced plastic and diecast metal in their make-up, the pressed steel being reserved for thc manufacture of the chassis.

PUBLIC TRANSPORT VEHICLES
There are many tin toys representing the well-known buses and trams which operate – or have operated – in many of the world's cities. Even the famous San

115

115
This 7in/18cm-long
tinplate model of the
famous San Francisco
cable car makes an
ideal souvenir for
visitors to the
Californian town. The
miniature cars were
originally produced in
Japan, but these more
recently available
examples were made
in Taiwan in the 1970s.
The cars move by
friction-drive, and
make a bell-ringing
sound as they travel
along.

116
Fine, Japanese-produced tinplate buses like this "Highway Express" friction-drive example by Nomura Toys were issued in the 1960s and '70s. Not yet too hard to find, this particular example measures 11in/28cm in length.

116

Francisco cable cars have been commemorated in tinplate to be sold as souvenirs of a visit to the city, usually carrying the message "Made in Japan."

British-style trolleybuses appeared in the toy shops in the 1950s and '60s, made by such firms as Wells-Brimtoy and Betal in the UK. They were aimed at the cheaper end of the market and were often fitted with the simple "piano-wire" spring mechanisms. One particular British-type miniature tinplate bus, by Wells-Brimtoy, had an ingenious clockwork mechanism which allowed it to stop and start during its journey, with a bell signaling "stop" and "go" just like the real vehicle! Normally, such toys were restricted to the simple luxury of mechanical forward movement. A large clockwork Betal toy was finished to represent either a double-decker bus or a trolley bus – the transformation effected by the simple addition of the trolleys. This vehicle also featured the luxury of electric illuminating headlights, working from a dry battery slung under the chassis. In the 1950s and '60s, the French firm of Joustra brought out a large clockwork Paris trolleybus with opening doors and a ringing bell.

The German firm of S Günthermann produced a single-decker touring bus, whose transparent roof boasted an opening ventilation panel. Another of their buses featured the Continental-style corridor trailer extension. Kellerman of Nuremberg produced another single-decker bus, carrying the logo "Deutsche Bundesbahn," and Tipp & Co offered a nicely turned-out single-decker luxury bus with a sliding roof panel.

In Japan, manufacturers turned out a great variety of buses, the majority designed in American style, with many carrying the logo of the famous Greyhound bus company. Japanese toy buses appeared in battery-operated versions, with clockwork motors, or were powered by "push-and-go" friction drive. A tinplate battery-operated "Old Time" London-style omnibus with an open top was marketed in the 1960s; it had working lights and incorporated the useful "bump-and-go" mechanism designed to turn the vehicle away from any obstruction it happened to run up against.

117

The British firm of Chad Valley included buses like this in their 1950s catalogs and they proved very popular toys. They were some 12in/30cm in length.

117

118
This is a fine representation of a motorcycle and side-car from the German firm of Tipp & Co and dates to the 1950s. The mechanism is clockwork and there is provision for a battery to be fitted underneath the side-car to provide headlight illumination. The toy is 7½/19cm long.

118

TINPLATE MOTORCYCLES

A popular theme with tinplate toy collectors is the motorcycle. There are fewer motorcycle toys around than cars, so the choice is more limited. The motorcycle featured minimally among pre-war tin toys and once manufacturing resumed in the late 1940s, tinplate motorcycles began once again to make an appearance in limited numbers.

Probably some of the best examples came from Tipp & Co of Germany. Their motorcycles, some with side-cars, were beautifully modeled to the firm's high pre-war standards. They came with clockwork or friction drives, some with steerable front forks. One model, although friction-powered, came with a working electric headlight. One variation of this model was issued as a police motorcyclist, with siren and winking red light.

Although Mettoy's toys closely resembled Tipp & Co products, their general quality tended to be somewhat inferior. However, Mettoy's motorcycle toys were generally colorful and, in 1951, a clockwork-powered model was introduced in two different styles with a Red Indian rider and with a clown rider. The lithography was different on each machine and on the figures within, their bodies being integrally molded with the rest of the toy and printed with suitable clothing. The Indian and clown heads, decorated and added later, were molded from composition. Other motor bike toys from Mettoy which appeared around the same period, included an all-tinplate pressing featuring a male driver. Lithography turned these models into a sporting motorcyclist and a police patrolman.

Two popular clockwork model motorcycles with side-cars, issued by Mettoy in the early 1950s, were also based on identical tin pressing. They were turned into either a clown or an Automobile Association patrol man by the lithographic process before leaving the factory! Though quite small, being only around 3 in (8 cm) in length, they were neatly produced toys.

120

Gebrüder Einfalt, the German toy company well known through its "Technofix" trademark, brought out a clockwork novelty motorcyclist toy in the 1950s which, when operating, would repeatedly fall over and right itself! Another example, with friction drive, left sparks behind as it traveled along, while a further friction-powered motorcycle could be purchased with, or without, a siren noise.

Schuco produced a number of novelty motorcycles, all neatly designed and made to the usual high standards one had grown to expect from this German firm of toy makers. "Curvo" was the most complicated piece because its ingenious mechanism allowed the owner to set the pattern its route would follow when the

119 120

These two tiny 3in/8cm-long clockwork motorcycles with side-cars came from Mettoy of England in the 1950s. Both pressings are identical although one has been lithographed to represent an Automobile Association patrol man and the other a clown.

119

mechanism was wound up and released. There was a choice of making the toy travel in a straight line, in a circle, in a square, and so on. Route patterns providing a total of seven geometrical journeys were available for selection at the turn of a knurled knob on the handlebars. "Mirakomot" was a similar sized toy with a mechanism which prevented the motorcyclist from riding off the edge of a table, while "Motodrill Clown" — basically the same tinplate pressing in its later version — manages to execute a sudden hair-raising spin. Then there is a motorcyclist called "Carl," designed to keel over realistically as he travels around a bend. Some of the models were reintroduced after World War II; others made their first appearance at that time. The earlier examples bear the legend "Made in US Zone," Germany; later models merely "Made in Western Germany."

The original "Motodrill Clown," incidentally, was from a different pressing. It featured a rider with a large, disproportionate clown's head. The later version changed, losing its clown figure, to become a variation of "Mirakomot," though retaining the original name. A similar figure — with a large head and a shock of hair, based on the German

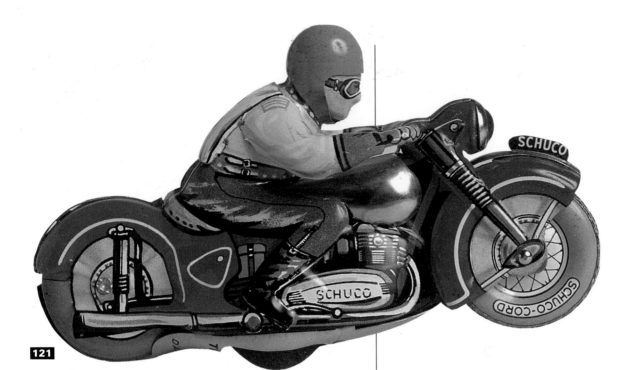

121

121
Schuco of Germany also produced "Motodrill Clown," a popular 1950s toy clockwork motorcycle which could travel along and suddenly spin off into a hair-raising skid before recovering to continue its journey. It is 5in/13cm long.

122
Schuco of Germany included this clockwork toy, named "Curvo," among their motorcycle range of the 1950s, all measuring around 5in/13cm in length. By means of the knurled knob above the front wheel-forks, this ingenious bike can be programmed to trace out a variety of patterned courses.

122

123

123
This is a most fascinating toy – a motorcycle with a driver who can actually mechanically mount and dismount in between riding his machine. It was produced by the German firm of Arnold in the immediate post-war years and named "Mac." Highly desirable, especially because of its most ingenious clockwork animation, the toy is 7½in/19cm in length.

124
Schuco's "Carl" is a clockwork motorcycle toy stamped from the same mold as "Curvo," although lithographed a little differently. Carl rides around in circles, animated by a simpler form of mechanism than Curvo. Dating from the 1950s, this toy is 5in/13cm in length.

124

story-book character "Strüwelpeter" – drove the "Mirako-Peter."

Perhaps one of the most famous toy tinplate motorcycles of all was that brought out by Karl Arnold of Nuremberg, Germany. This toy, marked "Made in the US Zone of Germany" appeared in the 1960s and was simply known as "Mac." Here we have a real piece of mini-automata because, in this case, the tin-plate driver has the ability to actually mount and dismount from his machine before and after riding! This is a marvelous toy, highly desirable and under-standably expensive. Its value varies, according to the color, some versions being rarer than others. But in any shade or hue, this is a toy which certainly rates high in the post-war collecting scene – and has little to rival it even in pre-war days. The Japanese copied its action during the height of the battery-operated novelty-toy boom in the 1960s and '70s, although in a much larger scale depicting a police patrol rider. The variation itself is a toy well worth looking out for.

A very rare variation of the Arnold "Mac" motorcycle toy features the same driver on a machine fitted with a side-car. Unfortunately the rider in this case stays seated otherwise, in countries where driving on the right is the rule of the road, he would be stepping on and off his bike into the side-car. Redesigning the mech-anism to allow the figure to operate on the machine's opposite side would,

obviously, have been a major expense, so seated he remains. This toy, produced in limited numbers in 1956, was created to commemorate the 50th Anniversary of the Arnold business.

125
Here is a real novelty – a clockwork motor-cycle ridden by a clown which breaks in two when it hits a solid object, effected by a simple release mechanism. This toy was made in the 1960s by Toplay of Japan and is 8½in/22cm long.

126

126

The Japanese firm of Bandai is noted for the quality of the toy motor vehicles they produced in the 1950s, especially their contemporary American limousines. This friction-drive 8in/20cm-long model of the Messerschmitt "Kabin Cruiser" is quite rare, as are other examples of miniature bubble cars of the period.

SCOOTERS AND BUBBLE CARS

Scooters also appeared on the two-wheeler scene. One German product featured a couple with a dog, riding along. Tinplate scooters of various qualities came from assorted manufacturers, the best of all being a fine model of a Zundapp "Bella," issued by Tipp & Co in the 1950s. Though two similar versions of this product were available, the hardest to find is the one featuring a driver who could give hand signals.

Another version of the German Zundapp "Bella" motor scooter was also originated by Gebrüder Einfalt of "Technofix." Pictured in the company's 1952 catalog, it was a much simpler toy featuring two riders — a male driver and female pillion passenger. The whole piece was integrally formed by the same metal pressing and provided with a simple friction-driving mechanism. In its simplicity it was a well-produced and attractively finished toy, certainly evocative of the bygone era of the motor scooter.

In the real world, the reign of the motor bike and scooter also saw the appearance of those mini-vehicles which became generally referred to as "Bubble Cars." It was inevitable that they would soon be marketed in toy form, and the best examples came from Japan. Friction-drive tinplate models of such vehicles as the Heinkel, Isetta, and the four-wheel BMW "put-putted" along many a floor. The fabulous Messerschmitt was not forgotten and, like the others, its model was finely detailed. Examples of all these are difficult to come by, since they were manufactured in limited quantities during a relatively short period.

There is plenty of scope for specialization in this section of the tin-toy world and there are collectors who concentrate upon buying commercial vehicle toys only. Other enthusiasts confine themselves to motor cars, while specialists accumulate miniature vehicles associated with favorite names in the motor engineering industry, or limit their collections to the products of one or two toy manufacturers. One American collector has built up a collection of postal vehicles from around the world, while several collectors reserve their attentions solely for examples from the Tri-ang Minic products. The choice is a personal one.

Ships, Boats and Aircraft

Seafarers must excuse toy collectors for not being aware of the difference between ships and boats, as they invariably class all model water-borne vessels as toy boats. As for flying machines, the pre-war interest in airships ceased to be reflected in post-war models, and the vogue for seaplanes passed, too. Toy-makers have concentrated their attention generally upon current aircraft, particularly those of the jet era, and the more modern helicopters. But, in general, tin boats and aircraft were less popular than other sorts of playthings and likewise, a decade or so ago, toy boats and aircraft were very low down on the list of fashionable collectibles – even the diecast model versions. Suddenly, the scene changed almost overnight. Both tinplate and diecast toy ships and planes became desirable, and the demand for examples has steadily increased over recent years.

SAILING AWAY

In the days of the ocean-going liners tin-plate models appeared more frequently on the market, as well as fine replicas of warships of the day. Earlier this century these toys were often magnificent – and expensive, of course, being available only to the sons of the wealthier classes. In addition to the more common clock-work models, there were steam-powered examples, and the odd one or two with pioneering electric motors. By the late 1930s the size of such toys had been much reduced. The 3ft-long (1m) "giants" disappeared from the toyshops forever. After the war German firms such as Fleischmann and Arnold reintroduced tinplate liners of simple design and powered by clockwork mechanisms. They were attractive models, representative of the smaller, cheaper toys generally made in the 1930s. They were designed to sail in the bath, or on the calm waters of a village pond. However, a number of toy boats were turned out as "carpet toys," designed to "sail" on wheels. These should probably be classed as novelty toys and do not usually appeal to true toy-boat collectors. Examples were issued from many of the world's toy makers, often cheaply produced, sometimes with mechanisms, more

127
This toy clockwork-powered liner made by Arnold of Germany dates from the 1950s, as the marking "Made in the US Zone" confirms. It is 12½in/32cm in length and designed to sail on water.

127

usually designed to be pulled along on a string. The cheaper speedboat models were favored by many of the world's toymakers.

Toy boats from Germany and the UK

In the 1950s the old-established German toy company of Fleischmann of Nuremberg was back in business with a catalog offering one of the best selections of toy boats. They ranged from a 7½in (19cm) long racing boat up to a 20½in (52cm) oil-tanker. Two other large models included a 21in (53cm) battle cruiser and a 15½in (39cm) torpedo boat. All these toys were clockwork-powered and were, for the period, quite impressively designed. Also available were a 19½in (50cm) long or a 17½in (45cm)

129

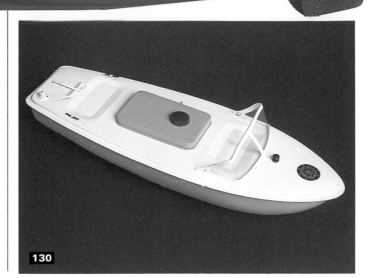

129
Victory Industries, a British company, produced this 13½in/34cm-long model of the "Miss England" speedboat in the 1950s. It is powered by a very simple water-circulating steam engine.

130
Sutcliffe toy boats were invariably quite simple, although well made. This British-made clockwork speedboat, the "Hawk," is 12in/30cm long and appeared in the 1970s.

128

128
This British-made toy boat was designed to operate on water. It represents the "Bluebird II" speedboat and is one of the more desirable collectors' pieces issued by Sutcliffe. It has a clockwork mechanism, is 13in/33cm in length, and dates from the 1950s.

long model of a two-funnelled luxury liner. Passenger ships ranged in length from 16in (40cm) down to 7½in (19cm). Eight different sizes altogether appear in the company's 1955 catalog.

Sutcliffe Pressings Ltd in the UK had specialized in toy-boat production since the 1920s. At that time they introduced a series of toy battleships propelled by either a clockwork mechanism or a simple heat-circulating system of the "pop-pop" type. Eventually all their products were clockwork driven, with the exception of the odd one or two models fitted with electric motors. The company resumed producing toy boats with the return of peace in the 1940s. A colorful range of well-made items proved popular sellers, especially at seaside holiday resorts.

A particularly popular Sutcliffe toy, especially among collectors, is the "Valiant" battleship. Produced as a "limited edition" towards the end of the 1970s, not long before the company closed down, this was a copy of one of the firm's original toys. Examples are still to be found in mint condition in their original boxes, probably never having been ailed. Sutcliffe boats soon find buyers whenever they appear on swapmeet stalls.

Lehmann, one of Germany's most prominent toymakers dating from the late 19th century, found themselves in East Germany after the war. However, the firm relocated to Nuremberg and began to specialize, as they had previously done, in producing novelty toys

They still used tinplate in their manufacturing, though plastic began to be used, too. Their toy mechanical boats were mainly produced with plastic bodies, though detailed models of a deep-sea fishing vessel and a tugboat were built from a combination of both materials.

Wells-Brimtoy of London included just one clockwork boat among their 1950s output of tinplate toys. This was a simple model of a paddle steamer which would thrash its way across the bathtub without difficulty!

More from Japan

The Japanese were highly active in the toy-boat market. There were battery-powered tugboats, liners, warships, and even a "Captain Kidd" pirate sailing ship which carried an open treasure chest revealing a mass of scintillating precious stones! A model ocean liner on wheels featured flashing lights and a realistically revolving radar scanner. Here again, the battery power could be harnessed to make the ship's siren sound, to add rolling movements, or cause smoke to issue from the funnels. Cheaply made small tinplate motor boats, of the "pop-pop" sort are ever popular and are still being produced from various sources of manufacture in the world to this very day.

131
This model tugboat, the "Neptune," is a product of MT of Japan and is 14in/36cm in length. Made in the 1950s, its electric motor with "bump-and-go" mechanism moves it around with a rocking motion, producing engine noises and the sound of a hooter.

132
The Japanese firm of Masudaya produced this 13½in/34cm-long "Pirate Ship" in the 1960s. The battery-powered toy runs on wheels and negotiates obstacles with its "mystery action," rocking realistically as though it were afloat, and emits the sounds of creaking timbers. There is an open treasure-chest on board and the "jewels" are illuminated. It is an unusual toy and hard to find at toy fairs nowadays.

131

133 — 136

These four cheap, currently produced "pop-pop" toy boats operate by means of a simple heat engine which can use a tiny candle or piece of solid fuel as a power source. Japanese-made, numbers 134 and 136 are of better quality than the other two. The yellow boat (133) is very crudely manufactured with sharp-edged metal and comes from India. The silver-colored boat (135) is of little better quality and orginates from Pakistan. Neither are safe as children's toys. They are approximately 6in/ 15cm each in length.

"POP-POP" VESSELS

The ever-popular "pop-pop" or "tock-tock" vessel was powered by a very simple form of steam engine. For many years these little tinplate vessels, often nicely lithographed, have provided inexpensive pleasure for children. The motor is simplicity in itself, a piece of U-shaped tubing with each end protruding, exhaust fashion, at the stern of the boat. When the tube is filled with water and heated at the U-turn, the steam generated "pop-pop's" out of the open tubing, propelling the vessel on its way. With each "pop" a vacuum is created which immediately is filled by more water, and so the process repeats itself until the heat supply, which may be nothing more than a tablet of solid fuel or a piece of birthday candle, runs out. Looping the tube around where it curves helps performance and some manufacturers also build in a small sealed tin "pan" device at the U-turn; this has the added effect of increasing the "pop-popping" noise and enhances the resemblance to the sound of a real motorboat.

The English toy-boat makers, Sutcliffe, used this type of simple water-circulating motor to power their toy battleships when they first entered the toy business in the 1920s. Their U-shaped tubing was curled spirally along its straight stretches, in an attempt to tone down the engine noise as much as possible – since the basic "pop-pop" sound was not really expected from a mighty ocean-going warship! Many firms have marketed the simpler, cheaply made, "pop-pops" since World War II and they are still being produced in the Far East, India, Pakistan, Eastern Europe, and Portugal.

137

This Japanese-made battery-powered toy ocean liner travels along with flashing lights, a siren and rotating radar scanner. Made by MT, it is 21in/53cm in length and dates from the 1960s.

138

The "SS Silver Mariner" is one of the marvelous Japanese battery toys from the 1950s to '60s. It carries four small tinplate military tanks in its hold and they can be loaded and unloaded by means of the ship's crane. The ship has a "bump-and-go" mechanism, flashing light, siren sound and is 15½in/40cm in length.

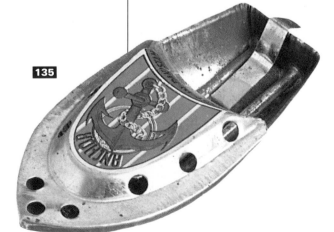

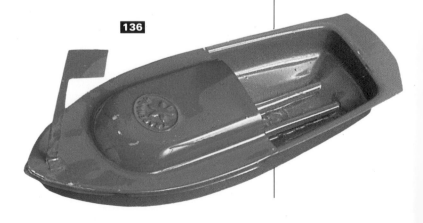

137

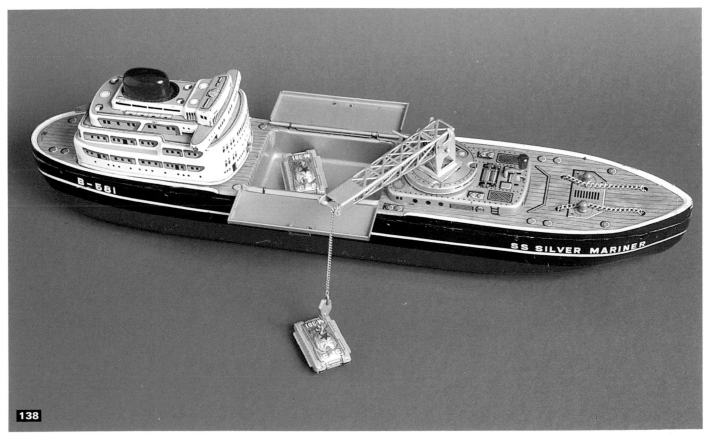

138

139

Submarine Collectibles

Among the Sutcliffe post-war range of toys were the "Nautilus" and "Sea Wolf," based upon their long-popular model submarine known as the "Unda Wunda." "Nautilus" was introduced in response to the interest in the Walt Disney movie of Jules Verne's novel *Twenty Thousand Leagues Under the Sea*.

A few other submarines were marketed around this time, some originating from Japan, while the German firm of Schuco brought out two similar models, part tin-plate, part plastic. One was battery-powered, the other had clockwork as a power source. A typical Japanese model submarine was driven by a flywheel mechanism set spinning by winding a handle on the deck. A British-made model with a similar mechanism, named "Nautilus," probably appeared in the shops around the same time as the Sutcliffe model of the same name.

139
This "Submarino," a 12in/30cm-long submarine made by Schuco of Germany in the 1960s to '70s, is battery-driven, although the firm also produced a similar clockwork-powered version. Both types had their power sources fitted in the removable plastic base which nests into the tinplate upper body of the vessel.

141

140
This "Nautilus" submarine is marked "Made in England," but bears no clue as to the manufacturer. It has a friction-drive mechanism operated by rapidly winding the projecting handle on the deck. It closely resembles a toy submarine which was produced in Japan and is undoubtedly influenced by the Disney film *20,000 Leagues Under the Sea.* It was made in the mid-1950s and is 10in/26cm in length.

141
Commemorating the Walt Disney movie *20,000 Leagues Under the Sea,* this well-made 6in/15cm-long clockwork toy submarine, "The Nautilus," was made by the British firm of Sutcliffe in the mid-1950s. Wind it up, place it in water, and it submerges until the power runs out and allows the boat to surface again.

140

142

TAKING TO THE AIR

Tinplate toy aircraft would obviously be far too heavy to ever fly, containing as they did a weighty mechanical motor or heavy batteries, if electrically powered. So the toymaker designed them with as much detail as possible and, as in the case of Japanese post-war tin toys, introduced in their make-up a variety of interesting eye-catching mechanical features – as "gimmicky" as those built into other types of toys. The majority of post-war toy planes which appeared on the market tended to reflect the design of their contemporary life-sized originals. Thus the market saw the appearance of a few World War II fighter planes, followed by various representations of the airliners of the day, and finally toy versions of the modern jet.

142

The modern jet age is represented in this excellent 1970s to '80s Chinese battery-operated model plane – a sleek "Supersonic Boeing 733," some 19½in/50cm in length.

143

Yone of Japan made this large (21in/53cm-long) "Turboprop Jet," a battery-powered airliner. The engines are illuminated when its props are revolving. It will taxi steadily along, after testing its engines in pairs, then move forward with all engines revving. It does not take off, naturally. When the engines stop and the plane comes to a halt, the passengers can be seen to move away from the windows and the door opens to reveal an air hostess. This novelty action is reversed as the plane moves off again.

143

144
Daiya of Japan introduced this impressive "Pan-Am Skyway Helicopter" on to the market in the 1960s. It is 8½in/21cm long and has friction-drive.

panel of lithographed metal illustrated with passengers' heads and shoulders automatically slides into view through the plane's windows, suggesting they had just taken their seats. In operation the aircraft taxies forward, halts, tests each engine in a realistic manner, and eventually revs up for take-off, although, of course, it never leaves the ground. This example is one of the best of the aircraft novelties and is also a reasonable replica of an airliner of the period. As a toy it is quite ingenious, an exceptional example of the design and workmanship of the Japanese toy industry.

Joustra, of France, was a company that placed several fine model aircraft on the market, including a superb tinplate flag-flying Air France "Croix de Sud" with revolving plastic propellers. About the same time, the German company, Schuco, issued battery-operated airliners in various well-known company liveries, all complete with remote cable steering. Novelties introduced by another German firm, Arnold, included at least two sizes of remote-controlled helicopters which flew in a realistic manner. A geared

From Airliners to Helicopters

Several appealing battery-operated models distinguish Japanese production of the 1950s to 1970s. They include forward taxiing planes with propellers turning, or jets screaming! One model features its air hostess closing the door and passengers taking their seats. A sliding

145
This cartoon-style futuristic toy is known as the "Bombardier Prop Fighter Plane" and is a product of WACO of Japan, probably dating from the 1960s. It is battery-operated, fitted with "mystery action" for by-passing obstacles, and is 10in/25cm long. The plane travels forwards with the propeller spinning, then stops, the cockpit-cover slowly opening to reveal the pilot. He moves his head and waves before the cover closes again and the plane resumes its journey. An engine sound is emitted and the engine lights up. The batteries are secreted in the tinplate 'pods' under the wings; in later models the pods were made of plastic.

145

winding handle at the end of a remote-control cable caused the rotor blades to revolve rapidly and thus lift the aircraft into the air. This was not strictly a tinplate toy, however, being necessarily made from lightweight aluminum with plastic rotors to surmount the weight problem. Nevertheless, it is an item which many collectors would be happy to accept into their collections, and refused by only the most ardent of purists.

In pre-war years many German manufacturers produced a variety of aircraft toys, but the factories that survived destruction to continue in business after 1945 tended to concentrate more on toy railways and motor vehicles, producing few toy planes, if any at all. Tipp & Co had marketed many fine tinplate aircraft in the 1930s and continued to supply many other fine tinplate toys in later years, but their post-war production favored plastic when it came to aircraft.

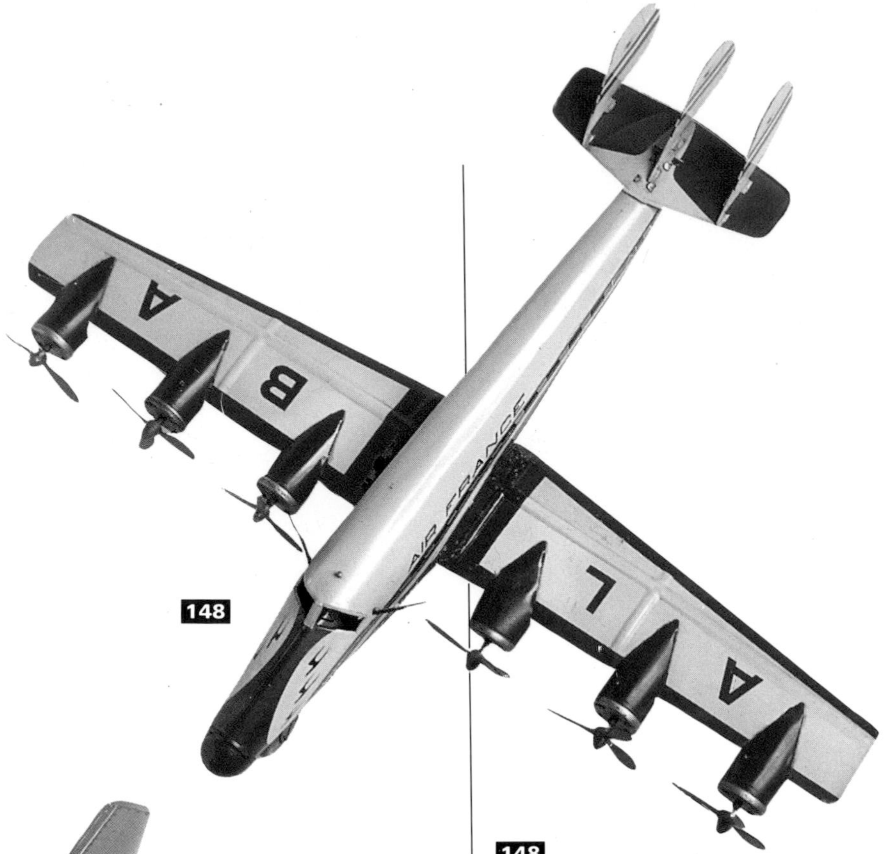

148

148
This impressive looking "Air France" six-engined airliner is all tinplate (including the flags flying from the cabin sides) apart from its plastic propellers. The clockwork mechanism wheels it along and turns the props as it goes. A red light beneath its nose can be illuminated from a battery. Made by Joustra of France in the early 1950s, the plane is 20½in/52cm in length.

146

147

146 147
The Schuco battery-powered "Elektro Radiant" Viscount airliner appeared in several airline liveries: the two examples illustrated carry the name of Lufthansa and the initials of the old

British Overseas Aircraft Corporation. These fine models, 15in/38cm long, were issued from 1957 to 1968 and also displayed the names of KLM, Sabena, Pan American Airlines and Swiss-Air.

149

are currently reintroducing limited editions of their 1930s' tin toys, among which is an excellent model seaplane.

Some track-toys feature aviation themes (see the chapter on Other Tinplate Toys for descriptions of other track toys). One of these is the German Technofix "International Airways" toy featuring a scenic tinplate layout with airports at either end. Between the two a plastic jet can be controlled to take off, circle around, and land at the neighboring airport – all done by wires. A great number of simple toys with planes circling around control towers, pylons, and over hangars have appeared on the market since World War II.

Miniature Planes

Smaller tinplate planes were produced in abundance in the post-war years, mostly free-wheeling or with simple friction drive. A few had clockwork motors. Jet planes were more common, because they were fashionable – and did not require the additional expense of propellers! There were miniature helicopters, too. Examples usually had revolving rotor blades geared to work from the wheels when the toy was pushed along or powered by a fly-wheel drive.

One popular small aircraft, currently produced in countries where tinplate toys are still being manufactured, is the little monoplane which somersaults as it moves along. This toy is invariably color-fully decorated, and is marketed as a "Circus Plane" or "Stunt Plane." It originates from many countries – including Germany, China, and Japan. Obviously, this toy needs a clockwork mechanism to make it perform.

Smallish low-winged fighter planes of World War II vintage are often found. Mettoy produced a camouflaged RAF version, while the Spanish manufacturer Paya made several aircraft, including a "Thunderbolt" of the US Army Air Force. Paya continued to make toy planes long after the war. Indeed, over recent years a number of toy aircraft have been produced by Paya. They are roughly 50 per cent tinplate and 50 per cent plastic, the lower half of the body and wings formed from tin, the upper half from plastic. Paya

149
Dating from the 1960s, this sturdy battery-operated "Jet Airliner" is a well-made toy from China, measuring 19in/49cm long.

150
This small 6in/15cm-long "Air Plane" has friction-drive and is a modern Chinese product.

150

151

151
This little clockwork plane, known as the "Training Plane" actually "loops the loop" – but without leaving the ground. Toys of this particular type have been issued by manufacturers of many countries from as early as the 1930s. This currently produced example is made in China, and is 4in/10cm long.

Toy and Model Trains

Toy trains followed the introduction of the railroad system which began to criss-cross countries in the early to mid-19th century. These early examples were marketed primarily as "scientific toys," designed to introduce their young owners to the wonders of the Steam Age. They were propelled by live steam, generated in their brass boilers from the heat of a spirit-burner fitted underneath. Tinplate trains were usually driven by clockwork power, this being a less messy alternative to steam for toys designed for the home. Electric motors were also used to a limited extent on some toy engines but clockwork was the main driving force for model locomotives for many years.

With the introduction of trains that could run along tracks just like the real railroad engines, the demand grew for all kinds of accessories to add realism to the layouts their owners constructed — stations, engine sheds, signals, and so on. Toy trains were more than just toys for children, they were working models to their fathers; a situation which certainly pleased the manufacturers — many a father has bought his son a toy simply as an excuse to enjoy playing with it himself!

Some wonderful examples of railroad locomotives in miniature were being produced early this century and various track widths were introduced, the most consistently popular being Gage 0. There were larger gages available too, but 0-gage was more suited to indoor use.

The majority of toy trains tended to only vaguely resemble any of the real-life locomotives. But there were exceptions. For example, Meccano Ltd of Liverpool, UK, who produced Hornby Trains, introduced a number of engines in the 1930s which were more accurately modeled and were therefore appreciated by boys who were keen railroad enthusiasts. The 0-gage "Princess Elizabeth" was one of these — the largest and best of the lot. Here was a real quality-product which the firm would never ever produce again — its price, five guineas (about $13), was just about double an average British working man's weekly wage at the time!

THE CHANGE TO SMALLER GAGES

The outbreak of World War II put an end to the production of such fine models — for good. When Meccano recommenced their toy business after the years of war work, the company promised to reissue many of their pre-war model locomotives. It was a promise they could never keep; only a few basic 0-4-0 models appeared, along with some rolling-stock, both goods and passenger, and a limited selection of accessories. The change was not just confined to Britain, it was also experienced by the French Hornby Company which had introduced a post-war

152

The phasing out of 0-gage by Hornby began in the late 1950s and this clockwork tender-locomotive, designated "No 50" by the makers, was one of the first to be removed from the production line. This loco, and its rolling stock, have survived in immaculate condition, a superb relic of the golden age of tin toys. The engine is 6½in/16cm long.

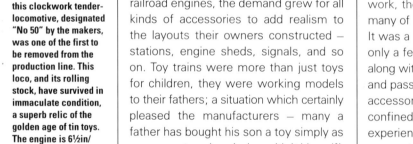

152

153

153 **154**

Hornby, produced by the Liverpool-based Meccano company, were eventually forced to serve the cheaper end of the toy trade, and this little 0-gage clockwork "M1" loco and tender set is a surviving example from the 1950s. The loco is 7in/18cm long. The attractively lithographed "Pullman" coaches came with the cheaper Hornby train sets.

155

This sturdily made 6½in/16cm-long Hornby "No 40 Tank Locomotive," with reversing clockwork mechanism, displays the "British Railways" lion logo of the 1950s. It is accompanied by one of the two "No 41" coaches which came with the boxed "No 41 Tank Passenger Train Set" together with a "Passenger Brake Van" and rails. The 0-gage loco is 6½in/16cm in length.

154

155

TRACK TOYS FEATURING TRAINS

Little railroad trains often featured in those colorful scenic track toys which originated mainly from Germany, many being produced by Technofix in the 1950s. Some of the smaller versions featured a small circular track around which the little train would travel, fixed to a hidden revolving tinplate disc, and surrounded by painted scenery, sometimes complete with a couple of tiny stations. One popular pre-war toy which was revived in the 1950s features a straight strip of track along which a tiny railroad engine travels, pulling a truck behind it. At the end, the locomotive swivels neatly around and begins pushing its truck back to the opposite end, where it swivels once more, hooking itself on to the truck and making the journey again – continuing until the clockwork motor runs out of power. There are variations on this toy, all fascinating to watch and many with extra ingenious actions.

156
This 14½in/37cm-long toy represents a straight stretch of railway track along which runs a tiny locomotive. It pushes a truck from one end to the other where it revolves and hooks back onto the truck automatically, before pulling it back to the opposite end of the track. Another revolution of the turntable allows the engine to start pushing the truck again – and so on until the clockwork needs rewinding. This is one of a few similar small track toys produced by the German firm of Arnold, both before and after World War II.

157

selection of tinplate engines, trucks, carriages, and accessories which were superior to those from their British parent company. Even in the United States toymakers were noticing a steady fall in sales of their toy railroads and it became apparent that a resistance was being built up against the 0-gage scale. It seemed that a smaller gage was required – and also that the children of the new era were more sophisticated and wanted toy locomotives which more accurately represented their full-size counterparts.

Meccano Limited had already turned over to the narrower 00-gage and had launched their smaller Hornby "Dublo" series just before the outbreak of war. In the United States the famous Lionel company failed to see the warning light in time, leaving the change to the smaller gage too late – and it was the same with American Flyer; both companies went out of business. Trix Twin Railways (originating in Germany and marketed by Bassett-Lowke in the UK) and other German makers turned over to H0-gage, which was similar to 0-gage in size. TTR was the abbreviation for the company's name, so called because two trains could be run independently on the same narrow-gage track.

The famous and old-established German company of Gebrüder Märklin has survived to this very day as a leader in small-gage model railroads. At the turn-of-the-century Märklin were famous for their range of high-quality toys, railroads in particular. Another German toy-railroad manufacturer was Karl Bub &

Co; in an attempt to stay in business they decided to abandon 0-gage and turned to the newly introduced S-gage, a sort of half-way scale between the 0- and 00-gages. Unfortunately S-gage failed to catch the public's imagination and Bub's mistake proved to be their downfall. It was the same with the French JEP company, whose change to S-gage proved equally disastrous.

Fleischmann, another well-known German firm of long standing, decided to concentrate on model-railroad production after the war. They carried on making 0-gage products with electric and clockwork motors, and mainly in typical German outline. Their locomotives appeared in both steam and electric styles, the latter fitted with overhead pantographs (although the electric current was actually picked up from the track and not from overhead wires). Originally the majority of their engines were four-wheeled, though the electric outline versions had six wheels. Fleischmann were eventually forced to follow the demand for smaller-scale trains and entered the H0-gage market, and their range included several models of the large Continental-style locomotives and a selection of American-type engines, specifically aimed at wooing the large potential market in the United States.

For really first-class railroad models Bassett-Lowke of Northampton was the company to turn to, their products were well made, well designed, and necessarily expensive. They had branches in various British cities and, in a way, were really

157
This superior-quality 9½in/24cm-long British-made model clockwork locomotive was made by Bassett-Lowke. Its name, "Prince Charles," dates the model as a 1950s product.

STEAM POWER

Real steam power was reserved for toy stationary steam engines, model railroads, and ships. For many years novelty toys were specially designed to be operated by a belt-drive running from the flywheel of a toy, stationary steam engine. Such toys were made well into the post-war years, mainly in West Germany.

Post-war steam-powered toys were less complex and usually smaller than their pre-war versions. Popular examples included a workman hammering on an anvil or sawing wood. Sometimes the figure was sheltered within a tinplate building, featuring a turning waterwheel. Other, less colorful pieces, were steam-powered machines only, without operators. The driving wheels were often fitted with a handle so they could be turned manually, as an alternative to fixing up a belt-drive to the steam engine. Occasionally, the belt-drive could lead to a separate inertia motor, taking its power from a rapidly-rotating heavy flywheel, or even from a free-standing battery-powered electric motor. Such toys were produced by various German toymakers and are not generally quite as expensive as their mechanical counterparts. But post-war versions were produced in relatively small quantities.

These fascinating toy steam engines are still commercially produced. Stationary engines are also collected, but not to such a great degree as other items of the toy world. They command more interest if they are an integral part of a model railroad locomotive or ship. Strictly speaking, they are not really tinplate toys, though tin toy fans often have a weakness for steam mechanisms.

a couple of trucks or carriages, and a circle of track. The box-lid invariably carried an impressive picture of a huge locomotive speeding along!

There were larger sets, too, to which had been added extra track to form an oval, a small station, signals, and maybe a tinplate tunnel. Some of these cheaper model engines were a little more detailed, such as the 4-4-0 blue liveried British Railways loco made by Chad Valley and the Mettoy 4-4-0 Schools Class "Eton." Not too many years ago such boxed sets were very hard to sell at toy fairs but today they are soon snapped up when they appear on a stall at a reasonable price. They really need to be in mint condition to be properly appreciated and they look well set-out in their original cartons.

One of the last companies to produce models in 0-gage was the Spanish firm of Paya, a company now operating as a co-operative and reissuing many of their earlier tinplate novelty toys in limited editions. The resurrection of the firm's 0-gage railroad models has helped bring pleasure to a new generation and revive nostalgic memories for the older one!

toyshops for grown-ups. In pre-war days the company also marketed German-made model railroads, and collectors still refer to "Bing for Bassett-Lowke locomotives." Their engines were available with clockwork or electric motors, the latter being much more convenient to handle on large layouts.

The smaller 00- and H0-gage locomotives ceased to be manufactured from tinplate, as diecasting the metal was found to give superior reproduction of detail at a lower cost. Some companies used modern plastics in place of metal. However, some companies continued to manufacture carriages and trucks from tinplate for some time.

0-GAGE SETS

Many cheaper 0-gage railroads were marketed by other manufacturers in the 1950s and '60s, such as Chad Valley, Wells-Brimtoy, Betal, and Mettoy. They were usually presented as boxed sets, the simplest set containing a clockwork engine and tender, or a tank engine with

158
Made by Mettoy in the 1950s, this is an interesting 0-gage train set of the cheaper variety. The set included this clockwork-powered streamlined engine and tender, shown with one of the coaches supplied; the set would have come complete with the customary circle of tinplate track. The loco is 6in/15cm long.

158

159

160

159 160

This 7½in/19cm-long "Eton" clockwork schools-class locomotive and tender were manufactured by the British firm of Mettoy in the 1950s. Not as well made as Hornby products, such 0-gage sets were produced to sell in a lower price range. The "Pullman" coach was designed by Mettoy to be pulled behind the "Eton" locomotive.

161
This simple 1960s novelty tin toy called the "Tinkling Locomotive" is 9½in/24cm in length and carries the Masutoku trademark. The legend on its box says "Battery Operated Locomotive Tinkles Fireman Moves his Head." The loco moves with "mystery action," and the engine's chimney and the driver's head are molded from plastic.

161

"CARPET" AND NOVELTY TOY TRAINS

"Carpet toy" trains are the sort designed to run on the floor, not on a track and, in pre-war days were either operated by clockwork or simply by pulling them along on a string. Many of their post-war equivalents originated from the thriving Japanese toy industry and came in all shapes and sorts. There were friction-driven and clockwork-powered models but, by far the most prevalent were the battery-driven toy trains, very often designed to the old American style, with cow-catchers, siren sounds, and so forth. This American type of train often featured an engineer leaning out of his cab, perhaps waving a lantern as the train traveled along, magically avoiding all obstacles standing in its path by means of its ingenious "bump-and-go" mechanism. Some of the examples even issued a mechanical clanking sound as the engine trundled along. They were invariably colorfully decorated and never intended to be taken too seriously, being toys pure and simple.

Some toy trains had funny faces lithographed on their smoke-box fronts, similar to the style of "Thomas the Tank Engine;" others traveled along in a peripatetic manner, while one curiosity could actually walk on four legs which replaced its wheels! These and other similar examples were definitely toys intended to amuse.

However, there are collectors for these examples just as there are for the more seriously modeled engines.

In the 1930s, when the American model railway manufacturing company of Lionel was facing bankruptcy, it was rescued by the successful sales of a money-spinning "Mickey Mouse" manual railroad truck. A similar toy had also been produced before the war by Wells-Brimtoy of London, featuring Mickey and Minnie Mouse. In the 1950s Wells-Brimtoy revived the toy, but with Donald Duck replacing Minnie. Still clockwork-powered, the toy had the two characters pumping away at the cross-lever as they trundled around a circle of 0-gage track. A rarer version was also produced with Gus and Jaq – the mice from the Walt Disney *Cinderella* movie – doing the pumping.

There is a worldwide preoccupation with model railroads. In fact, the hobby is so popular that many of the early surviving examples are now in specialized collections, effectively removing many interesting examples from general circulation. Therefore, fewer pieces appear at toy collectors' fairs and swapmeets than were to be found a decade or so ago, and when they do surface prices are correspondingly high. However, there is hardly a collectors' toy fair which does not have at least one or two model-railroad specialists present – and interesting items can, of course, pop up on any stall.

162

162
This 7in/18cm-long novelty American-style train carries on its box the fanciful name of the "Atchison, Topeka & Santa Fe" railway company of America. When the clockwork motor is wound up, the toy shakes and clicks its way along the floor. The plastic funnel indicates that it is a later Japanese product; it was produced by Yoneya Toys in the late 1960s to '70s. It is decorated with colorful lithography, and a comical face appears on the smoke-box door.

Robots and Space Toys

Among the vast output of tin toys which issued from Japanese manufacturers in the early post-war era was a great variety of fantasy products. These included science-fiction-style robots, as well as astronauts and a number of imaginative space vehicles, from rocketships to flying saucers. Today such sci-fi toys have come into demand internationally, with some collectors interested in nothing else. Many fine examples, especially robots, can realize amazingly high prices, the rarer ones often commanding four-figure sums when they appear in auction. The robots and space toys must all possess a common feature to guarantee interest from collectors – they must be products of the imagination. Items based on real-life science and space exploration are definitely out.

SPACECRAFT
Some early examples include the 1940s "Space Rocket" issued by Günthermann

SPACE TANKS

163

163 164
Both these battery-operated sci-fi vehicles have been named "Space Tank" by their different manufacturers. The first example, made by Nomura Toys of Japan, is fitted with the ubiquitous "bump-and-go" mechanism found in so many Japanese toy vehicles. It dates to the 1960s and is 7in/18cm long. The second example dates from the 1970s and was made in China. The robot driver has moving arms, and the 11in/28cm-long tank is equipped with flashing lights and caterpillar tracks which enable it to negotiate small obstacles.

164

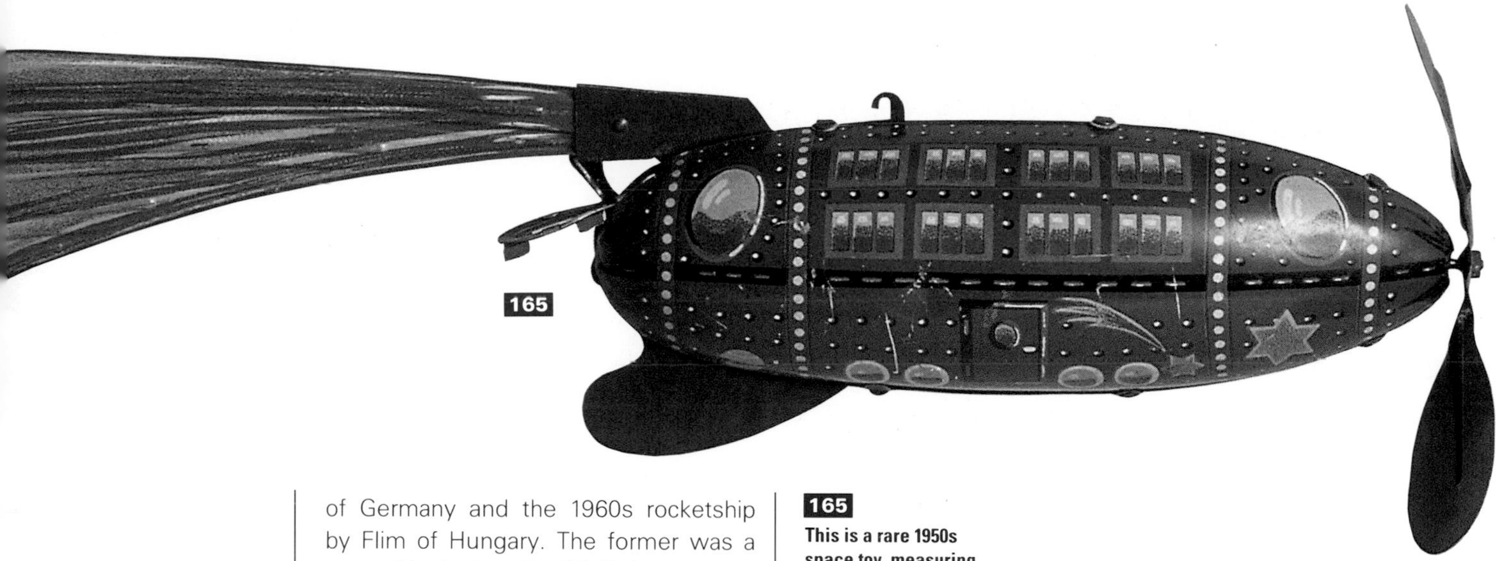

of Germany and the 1960s rocketship by Flim of Hungary. The former was a spaceship designed to "fly" along a steel-tape hooked up to a wall, issuing sparks from its tail as it sped along. An ingenious mechanism allows it to release a para-chutist, which then slides down the tape. The Hungarian space vehicle travels forward by friction drive and when its nose hits an object, the rocketship stands up vertically, apparently ready for take-off.

The Günthermann 1957 catalog includes a mention of only one space toy, a tinplate mechanical "Flying Rocket" which could be made to fly in a circle, hanging by a short length of string from the end of a hand-held stick. It had a "futuristic" appearance, sporting a pair of swept-back stubby wings, and was propeller-driven from the front by its clockwork motor. Various rocket toys were produced by other manufacturers worldwide, the majority of the models being earth-bound, their movement confined to traveling on wheels. Some examples were propelled like missiles

165

This is a rare 1950s space toy, measuring 13½in/34cm long, which carries no maker's mark or details of the country of origin. It is futuristic in design, a real fantasy toy with a detachable tinplate fiery tail (often missing from surviving examples). When dangled from a string, its clockwork motor will turn the propeller fast enough to make the rocketship "fly," and an internal flint mechanism ejects a spray of sparks from the rear.

166

This 9in/22cm-long clockwork fish-like "Pioneer" space vehicle is something of a rarity – and one of the most curious toys of its type. It dates from the 1950s and was produced by Kanto (trademark KO) of Japan.

167

167
A variation on the theme of the track toy and of special appeal to the space-minded, this futuristic space toy features excellent colorful lithography. "Space Port," 14½in/ 37cm long, was made in the 1950s to '60s by the German company that produced many track toys, Gebrüder Einfalt – better known by their "Technofix" trademark. The little clockwork space ships loop around the vertical track, circling the Earth as they go.

168
Flying saucers are especially popular with collectors who are fascinated by fantasy space toys. They were produced in many sizes and with a variety of actions, the battery-operated ones providing the best performance value in terms of strange noises and flashing lights. Marked "Made in Japan," the exact origin of this appealingly designed and lithographed flying saucer is not known, although it was possibly made in the 1960s. It is 6½in/17cm in length and fitted with a friction-drive mechanism.

168

from a gun by a spring mechanism — and tended to be frowned upon by safety-conscious parents!

The Japanese were responsible for many spacecraft, along with a wide selection of flying saucers. These usually travelled along winking their colored lights and issuing strange "space" sounds. Their astronauts differed from robots mainly by having a human face peering out of a space helmet, although they often carried out quite similar actions; they could walk and even fire space weapons. The German firm of Technofix introduced a kind of track-toy called "Spaceport" in which two spaceships travel in orbit around the Earth's globe.

UFOs were generally well represented by a multitude of bizarre "flying saucer" vehicles, the battery-operated versions being particularly active in novelty performance, complete with arrays of blinking colored lights and the shrieking noises with which our imagination associates these mysterious machines from outer space. Inevitably this range of toys, whether battery-operated or not, was the subject of colorful and decorative lithography, giving them a special charm.

In the 1950s Wells-Brimtoy, the British toy manufacturing concern, marketed a 7½in (19cm) long tinplate Space Ship. It was a floor-runner, having two clockwork-driven side wheels and an aircraft-type nose wheel. As it traveled along, flint-produced sparks were emitted from its tail. It was grandly advertised as having a "Gyroscopic Sparking Mechanism!" Its lithography included a series of oval windows along each side revealing a full complement of passengers.

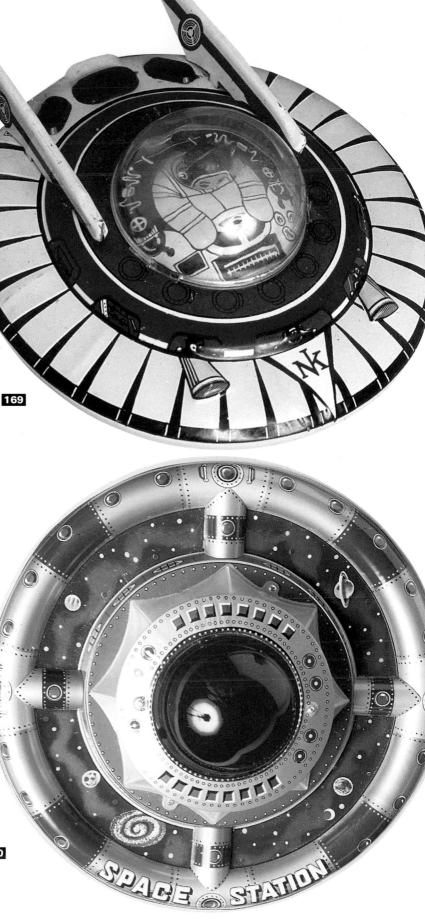

169

169
This flying saucer is a present-day product from China. It is 5½in/14cm long, runs along by friction-drive and issues a shower of sparks from a flint mechanism.

170
This Japanese-made "Space Station" has friction-drive and is 6½in/17cm in diameter. It bears no trademark, but originates from the 1960s to '70s.

170

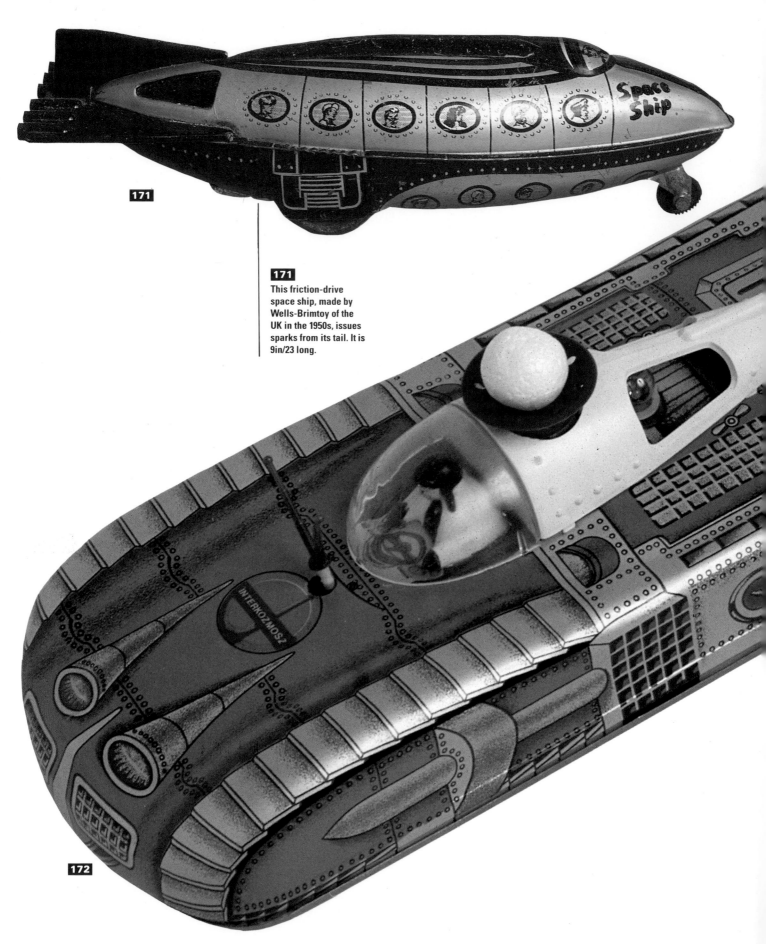

171

171
This friction-drive
space ship, made by
Wells-Brimtoy of the
UK in the 1950s, issues
sparks from its tail. It is
9in/23 long.

172

CALLING ALL ROBOTS

Robots were invariably well designed and obviously the products of fertile imagination. They came in all shapes and sizes, fitted with mechanisms ranging from the simple to the amazingly ingenious. One of the most eagerly sought-after robots is "Mr Atomic," produced in Japan for the American company Cragstan. There are two known color variations of this particularly hard-to-find toy and both are able to hum a simple computerized tune when the power is switched on.

Another highly desirable and difficult-to-find toy is the "Purple Target Robot," which has a most curious action. It came supplied with a dart-firing gun and the idea was to shoot at the robot. Scoring a hit stopped the automaton advancing and it would turn away, only to suddenly swing round to advance again on its attacker, issuing terrible electronic screams. "Shoot him – he roars, flashes, and goes away – soon comes back to you!," announces the legend on the box-lid, in the typical imperfect Japanese-English of the day.

172
This sci-fi space vehicle is named "Holdauto" by its Hungarian manufacturers. Battery-powered, it travels along carrying with it a lightweight ball suspended above the vehicle by a jet of air. The toy was made in the 1980s and is 12½in/32cm long.

ELECTRIC MOTORS

Electric motors have been used by toy-makers since the early days of this century, though not on a wide scale. They powered the odd toy ship and the occasional motor car. Later, model railroads were powered by electricity, which presented none of the problems of the early storage batteries. The current was transmitted directly from the mains supply, via a transformer along the metal track to be picked up by the motorized locomotive, as is still done today.

Improvements in dry battery manufacture meant that electric motors were occasionally tried out in toys in the 1930s, but it was Japanese designers who developed the potential of battery-operated toys and produced them on a big scale in the 1950s. Practically the entire massive output of such toys from Japan was of novelty appeal – even the ships, planes, trains, and all the animated figures. Many contained clockwork motors, others friction or inertia mechanisms, and a good percentage of the products were operated from ordinary flashlight batteries.

The beauty of such electrically-powered playthings was that extra effects could be included in a toy's repertoire. Besides movement, the item could be equipped with flashing colored lights, electronic sounds – even speech – and a replica steam locomotive or boat could have smoke coming out of its funnel. Smoke, created by heating machine oil contained in a metal capsule, was also used to imitate exhaust fumes from toy cars.

173

"Radicon Robot" had the luxury of possessing a simple, battery-operated remote-control system operated from a separate unit. The announcement on the box-lid claims it to be "The First and Only Complete Radicon Remote Control Toy." It is interesting to note that the same manufacturer also issued a "Radicon" toy bus and a "Radicon" toy speedboat, both with similar operation.

A highly collectible toy was based upon the character "Robby the Robot," which became popular through the Hollywood science-fiction movie starring Walter Pigeon and Anne Francis, entitled *The Forbidden Planet*. The film was based on William Shakespeare's play *The Tempest* and Robby replaced the original character of Caliban. This film-star robot was to reappear a little later in another movie, *The Invisible Boy*. Various models of "Robby" were marketed at the time, including "Robby Space Patrol," a curious contraption and a cross between a robot and a space buggy.

A small silvery clockwork robot was marketed from Germany in the 1950s. Named "Robot ST1," the manufacturer's name was given as "Strenco." Although it claimed to be "Made in Western Germany," this robot looks suspiciously as though it was produced in Japan. The separate four-wheeled truck which it pushed was an exact replica of a similar vehicle marked "Made in Japan," though decorated quite differently. "The Atomic Robot Man" is another smaller robot which looks as though it could have successfully auditioned for the part of the Tin Man in *The Wizard of Oz*. He resembles an early walking gas-meter, with dials on his body, one being that of a large analogue clock face, always showing the time to be around twenty minutes past one o'clock. It would not be easy for this particular Mr Atomic to tell the time by it, unless he faced a mirror and read it in reverse!

Other scarce examples are "Machine Man" and "Sonic Robot," which have very similar bodies but different heads, lithography, and actions. Rare, too, is "X-70," which has a dome-shaped head that can open like a budding flower to reveal a rotating television camera.

174

175

173
"Dino Robot" is 11in/28cm tall, battery-operated and has the unusual ability to open his headpiece to show that he is really a dinosaur in robot disguise. This rare toy, made in Japan in the 1950s to '60s, is a desirable piece among specialist collectors.

174
This 6½in/17cm tall robot dates from the 1950s to '60s and is Japanese-made, although the identity of the actual manufacturer is uncertain. Clockwork-powered, he walks forward, with a flint mechanism producing sparks in the holes which serve as eyes.

175
Currently marketed, this battery-operated toy is known as "Space Walk Man." The 12in/31cm-tall robot walks along, the doors in his chest opening intermittently to fire hidden guns. The tinplate robot is made in China in the Japanese style of earlier post-war years.

ROBOTS IN REPLICA

176 — 178

In the 1980s, a series of limited-edition ceramic copies of the rarer post-war Japanese tin toy robots were marketed to meet the upsurge in interest in this particular collecting field. Several of these numbered examples are illustrated here, all closely resembling their battery-operated originals which now realize three- and four-figure sums in specialized auction sales. Unfortunately, the company responsible for the ceramics went into liquidation before completing its intended range.

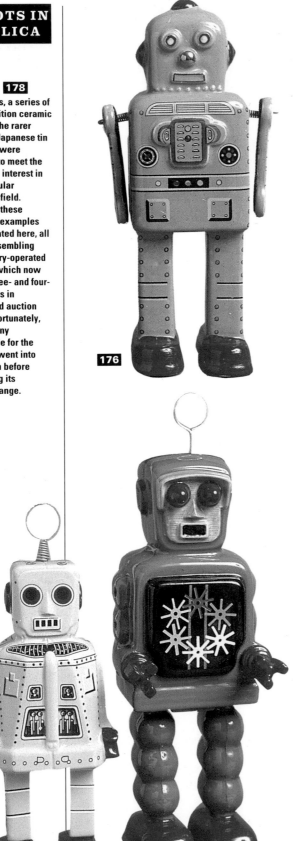

176

177

178

Another similarly designed example is "Dino," a real weirdo of a robot which can walk, and allows its robot head to hinge open to reveal a red-colored illuminated creature's head (which looks like a dinosaur's — hence, perhaps, the name "Dino") with a moving, growling mouth.

The "Smoking Spaceman" robot walks and emits smoke from his mouth while blinking his eyes, and the battery-powered "Talking Robot" moves along by friction drive. A push-button causes the figure to make various random statements, such as "Goodbye boys, I'm off to explore the universe." Of similar appearance is the toy robot known as "Chief Smokey," described as "Puffing Steam-like Smoke" and possessing "Lighted See-Through Action." "Mr Mercury" is a robot which obviously belongs to the same family. Though he has a remote-controlled walking action, he is actually operated by a couple of tiny green men working the controls inside his head!

The "Space Scout" is actually an astronaut. While he resembles a robot, the human face peering from the helmet classifies the toy as an astronaut. He can open a door in his chest which reveals a flashing, shooting gun — a feature possessed by a number of Japanese-made robots.

Many robots have plastic-fronted chests which reveal colorful gear wheels revolving as the robot advances. Some show similar curious machinery operating in their transparent craniums — one model boasts operating pistons where its brain should be. Others have TV screens in their chests, usually depicting scenes in outer space. One well-armed robot is "Rocket Man," a remote-controlled figure who is, as the box-lid attests, attired in "space armour" and "Walks and Fires Rockets at Your Command."

Robots are still being made, even in the middle of the present "Plastic Age," although their actions nowadays are pretty basic and no longer as bizarre as those of their predecessors. Many of the earlier robots also included plastic in their make-up, but were balanced by tinplate to classify them as tinplate toys. Plastic material won in the end, however, and it finally took over completely, except for the clockwork mechanisms.

The British-conceived robots, "the Daleks," from the BBC-TV series *Dr Who* have enjoyed international respect from science-fiction fans. The majority of toy Daleks are molded from plastic, and many are manufactured by Marx. One tinplate, clockwork-powered Dalek exists, however, incorporating some plastic in its make-up — and it was marketed for a short time by the British firm Cowan-de-Groot under their better-known trademark "Codeg."

The Japanese had also produced a range of battery-operated robot-style automata based upon mythical creatures from their culture; strange figural toys often referred to as "Shoguns" by their specialist collectors. For the most part they are fantasy Samurai warriors whom, legend decrees, direct their fearsome attacks against any invaders threatening the security of their homeland. There were also toys in the form of many of the "sci-fi" figures from their own movie and comic-book industry — including a number of prehistoric creatures, the most widely known being "Godzilla."

179
This is a relatively common type of Japanese battery-operated walking robot, which has the ability to display space pictures on its chest-mounted TV screen. This 8½in/22cm-tall model is fitted with molded plastic arms which date it to the 1960s to '70s.

180
As BBC television's "Dr Who" became known across the Atlantic, interest in related character toys increased, with a growing number of fans in the United States. Most of these toys were produced in plastic, but this rather rare "Dalek" is a tinplate clockwork-powered toy incorporating only a small amount of plastic material. It is 5in/13cm high and was made by the British firm, Cowan de Groot, trading under the name Codeg, in the 1950s to '60s.

181
This page from a trade leaflet issued by Bullmark of Japan, illustrates their tinplate version of the favorite Japanese movie monster "Godzilla" (see the chapter on Character Toys for a photograph on the actual toy), and also the strange robot-type "Shogun" figures which were primarily produced for the home market in the 1950s to '60s.

179

180

FROM THE B B C
TELEVISION SERIES

★ STRONG
CLOCKWORK

● REALISTIC
ACTION

MECHANICAL
DALEK

© BBCtv 1965
MADE IN ENGLAND

MADE IN GT. BRITAIN

カッコイイ！
ウルトラマンがお部屋１ぱいにとび廻ります

B/Oウルトラマン
（特大）

1,450：1,530

ゼンマイ仕掛けで
ノシノシよく歩きます
ゼンマイウルトラセブン 550：600

ゴジラ
○：1,420

眼が光り、胸の
カラータイマー
が音をたて点滅
する、そして歩く

ゼンマイウルトラマン
550：600

眼が光り
手を振りながら
ノシノシ歩く

クルッと後ろに大回転

ズ

仮 **181** ダー 1,250：1,310

B/Oウルトラセブン 1,200：1,260

B/Oウルトラマン 1,200：1,260

怪獣空中大回転！
アクロバット怪獣 "ダンガー" 1,200：1,260

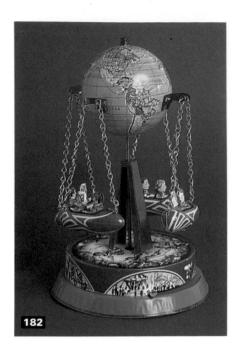

182

182
This 8in/20cm-tall clockwork merry-go-round is a current Chinese replica of a pre-war German Blomer & Schüler toy; topographical names on the rotating globe are still printed in German.

183
The Spanish tin toy manufacturer, Paya, began remanufacturing a series of their earlier toys in the late 1980s in limited runs. This 14in/35cm-long mechanical rowing boat is a good example of their products, which include motor cars, trains, and even "penny toys."

PRESENT-DAY REISSUES OF POST-WAR TIN TOYS

Many of the old familiar toy-makers' names are still in existence in the manufacturing world, though their products have usually changed considerably. The British firms of Chad Valley and Tri-ang, for example, still operate, though they no longer produce tin toys. Famous names are often purchased when their original owners cease trading, so we still have our Hornby trains, but they are no longer made by Meccano. As for the famous Meccano construction system itself, the name is now owned by a French company.

"Schuco" Toys from GAMA
The famous logo of Schuco lives on, now owned by the German firm of Georg Adam Mangold, still named after the man who founded the company in 1882. From his initials comes the company trademark GAMA. Today GAMA market a limited selection of the old, and once very popular, Schuco tin clockwork toys. These include the Schuco "Oldtimer" range of veteran car models originally introduced in the 1960s (see the chapter on Tin Toy Motor Vehicles): the Opel Doktor-Wagen, the Renault 6CV Voiturette, the old Model "T" Ford, and the Mercedes-Simplex. The Opel Doktor-Wagen is offered for sale both with and without an automatically raising canopy powered from the clockwork motor. The firm's revivals of some of the earlier popular tinplate Schuco products – all fitted with ingenious clockwork mechanisms – include the old favorite "Studio" Mercedes racing car; the "Examico 4001," which has four forward gears, neutral, and reverse; and the "Akustico 2002," a car similar in design but with a sounding horn instead of gears.

GAMA have also issued a boxed Schuco "Studio" kit and are expected to issue other examples of the old manufacturer's once-popular toys, using the original machinery from Schreyer & Co which they acquired.

Paya of Spain
Another company is doing good business from reintroducing toys they made in pre-war days. Using the original machinery, which had been stored away and found to be still in good working order, the Spanish firm of Paya restored its fortunes after having its fair share of business worries. Paya now operates as a workers' co-operative, still at their old factory in Ibi, near Alicante. In the past they made some splendid tin toys in an attempt to offset some of the flood of play-things pouring in from Germany, which threatened Spain's national economy. Today, with the realization of the worldwide interest in toy collecting, they have entered the "limited edition" business, turning out toys for collectors who cannot find – or afford – the real thing. These reissues range from a large tinplate clockwork-driven model of a Bugatti-style racing car, to a selection of smaller toys which include other automobiles and a number of simple, but attractive, little "penny" toys.

183

184 — 188
The Schuco "Oldtimer" range of clockwork-powered veteran car models, first produced in the 1960s, are currently being reissued by Georg Adam Mangold (GAMA) of Germany, using the original Schuco machinery. Illustrated here are: 184 and 185, the Opel Doktor-Wagen of 1909, both without and with an automatically raising canopy (7in/18cm long); 186, the Renault 6CV Voiturette of 1911 (6½in/16cm long); 187, the Mercedex-Simplex of 1902 (9½in/24cm long); and 188, the Model "T" Ford of 1917 (6½in/16cm long).

184

185

188

186

187

189 190
Two other Schuco cars reissued by GAMA are the "Akustico 2002" (189), which features four forward gears, neutral and reverse; and the "Examico 4001" (190), which has a sounding horn instead of the gear-action. Both models are clockwork-powered and are 5½in/14.5cm long.

190

189

191
GAMA have also reissued the famous Schuco "Studio" Mercedes racing car. This 5½in/14cm-long clockwork toy car was originally introduced by Schuco in the 1930s, and was marketed again following World War II. The "Studio" is steerable and features a jack and wrenches for removing the hubs, and a lever to remove the tires from the wheels.

191

Other Tinplate Toys

192

This 1960s track toy, carrying the "Technofix" trademark of the German firm Gebrüder Einfalt, consists of three racing cars traveling along two routes around the scenic lithographed tinplate trackwork. The ridged endless belt, powered by a clockwork motor positioned at the topmost point, carries the cars up the incline from where they freewheel down the course. The track base is 19in/49cm wide.

In addition to the obvious novelties, and rail, boat, air, and space toys, many other tinplate playthings were produced from the late 1940s onwards. They ruled the playroom until they were finally ousted by plastic products.

TRACK TOYS

Track toys are most attractive and usually have a great deal of interesting lithography on molded tinplate, which imitates the mountain scenery through which the miniature motor cars, buses, trains, or trams travel. Often these vehicles travel on a flat scene-painted tray, though buildings are usually three-dimensional.

Occasionally, the mountain scenes offer the bonus of a working cable-car system, heading up into the mountains. Other variations include street scenes. One Technofix product operates a system which stops the traffic of miniature tin cars while a tinplate family crosses the road. An English-made example has a cleverly designed track circuit which deceives the eye – a traveling car enters a tunneled intersection and mysteriously emerges from a most unexpected exit. The covered section can be hinged upwards to reveal the simple geometry of the track design which causes the illusion.

The German firm of Arnold also designed a series of small track toys in which vehicles were transported along a short stretch of track by means of an endless belt hidden beneath the track, down the center of which ran a long slot to permit the passage of the connecting link. At each end of the track the vehicle would spin around and return, traveling thus until the mechanism lost power. This toy existed in pre-war days and was

193

Only part of this 46½in/118cm-long track toy, produced by "Technofix" in the 1960s, can be shown in this photograph in order to display the lithographic detail to best advantage. The track base is hinged in two places so that it can be folded and stored in its colorful box. There are two tracks – one for the tramway system, the other for the two cars. Where the tracks cross, the clockwork-powered vehicles ingeniously come to a halt to allow the tram to pass without collision.

192

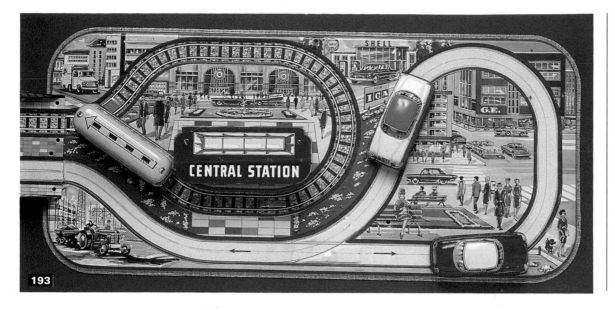

This simple track toy was produced by Arnold of Germany in the 1950s. The inertia created by the speed of the looping clockwork car kept it glued to its track during its "wall of death" style journey. The diameter of the circular track is approximately 9½in/24cm.

193

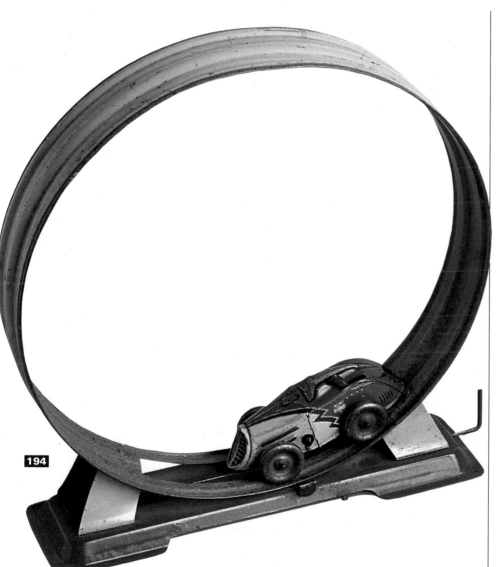

194

reintroduced in the late 1940s in various guises, the commonest perhaps being in the form of a railroad track with a tiny locomotive pulling a coach. At the extremities, the loco would spin around, detach itself from the coach, and push it back to the beginning, then turn again to reconnect – and so on.

A quite complex example from Technofix entitled "Country Tour" has roadways with road traffic and a miniature train. At X-crossings the traffic automatically halts to let the train go by. Another inventive model includes a tinplate camper, who pops out of his tent, and a boat crossing a tinplate lake. Yet another version represents a working coal-mine with pit-head winding gear at one end and a "steam-powered" engine room – with chimney – at the other. The track slopes upward from the pit-head and, between the two buildings, a workman takes a truck up and down the slope as long as the clockwork motor allows.

A much rarer toy is the circus act whose clown, "Lucky," walks along a tightrope stretched between two pylons. His movement is still transmitted from the hidden endless belt but here connected by a length of wire working along the slotted base of the toy.

Examples of track toys are currently reasonably easy to find and, curiously enough, seem to be generally in first-class condition, usually still in their original boxes. Often they are not quite as easy

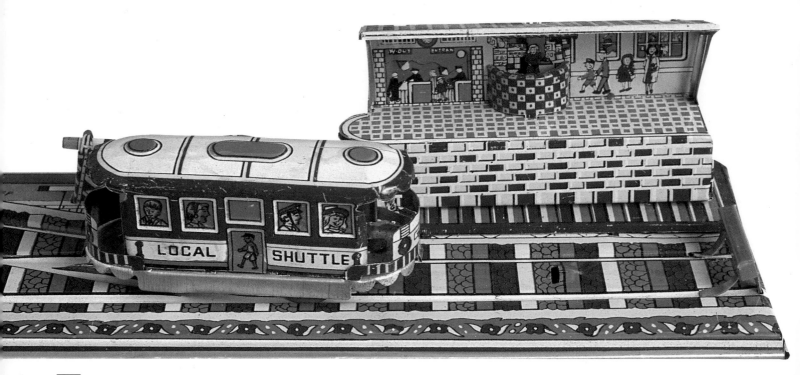

195

195
This novelty track toy is a present-day product from India and although colorful is rather crudely made. Called "Local Shuttle," it depicts a clockwork railroad traveling backwards and forwards along a short stretch of track between two little railroad stations which both, curiously enough, display the sign "Delhi." The coach is 4in/10cm long.

196

to display as the smaller toys, and this probably affected their demand until relatively recently.

TINPLATE TOWN TO TINPLATE KITCHEN

A few tinplate doll's houses with plastic furniture, and several garages from various makers came and went, while tin cooking ranges, complete with utensils, were marketed by the toymakers of many countries. In the early 1950s Mettoy in the UK brought out an attractive fully furnished tinplate doll's house, whose attached garage contained a family car. In the 1950s, Mettoy also marketed the "Joytown" Fire Station, a "Flying Squad" Station, and a Service Station. All three items were typically furnished and fitted with sliding doors for speedy vehicular access. The Fire Station included a clockwork fire engine, while an

197

196
Doll's houses have traditionally been constructed of wood, and tinplate houses and other buildings are relatively rare products of the toy world. This large tin house, measuring 23in/58cm across (including the built-on garage), was produced by Mettoy in the UK in the 1950s to '60s.

ambulance came with the police version. The Service Station was supplied with two clockwork cars. Later, in the 1960s, the company introduced more tinplate houses onto the market, including two doll's houses hinged to fold flat for packing and storage, as well as a suburban and a country house.

In the post-war years the majority of metal buildings were usually confined to model railroad stations and other buildings designed to complement railroad layouts, though these were generally much simpler products than their pre-war counterparts. The larger models went out with the decline of 0-gage and the smaller-scale examples were more easily produced from diecast metal.

In the UK Wells-Brimtoy marketed a push-along tinplate "Clucking Chicken" with flapping wings. It was propelled on wheels and mounted at the end of a stick. They also produced simpler push-along toys of similar character advertised as "Roller Chimes," since they jangled as the kiddies pushed them along. They also manufactured a variety of toy kitchen cooking ranges, the best examples being fitted with electric lights to give a fire effect. These were accompanied by a supply of kitchen utensils — pans, trays, graters, and plates — the kind of acces-

197
This 11in/28cm-wide tinplate bungalow was made by Marx in the 1950s, and is suitably lithographed inside and out.

198

199

198
If tinplate houses and bungalows are scarce, then this Mettoy "General Hospital" must be virtually unique. Again dating from the 1950s to '60s, the hospital measures 24½in/62cm across.

199
Tinplate vehicle stations of various kinds were produced in greater numbers than houses. This tinplate fire-station set, made by Mettoy in the 1950s, is equipped with a clockwork-powered fire engine and a friction-drive fire chief's car. Both vehicles measure round 6in/15cm in length.

sories traditionally included with such toys for many years. There was also a toy gas stove available. Weighing scales of varying degrees of quality were popular, too, from basic objects simply stamped out in tin to quite accurately designed miniature reproductions of the shop scales of the period.

Young girls were further encouraged to identify with domestic roles by the sale of tinplate toy carpet-sweepers decorated with colorful illustrations from the Walt Disney movie "Cinderella." Wells-Brimtoy made toy telephones too, as did other toy companies. Their version had a working dial geared to a bell which made a ringing sound as the dial returned to start. Toy tinplate guns appeared in the post-war era, always a popular toy with the boys – especially the ones which fired explosive caps. Some of these had attractive decoration added; those featuring space or cartoon characters, or representing space guns, have a special appeal.

GAMES AND PASTIMES

Table games were sometimes equipped with attractively lithographed tinplate playing boards instead of the more usual cardboard type. If such boards display illustrations of recognized character figures like Mickey Mouse, for instance, then so much the better. The same applies to pin-ball table games, some of which were produced to celebrate movie characters such as Batman or Superman.

200

The "Merry Builders," produced by the British firm of Cowan de Groot in the 1950s, is a simple gravity tinplate toy worked by the action of falling sand. Dry sand falls from the hopper at the top of the building into the hod on the topmost worker's back, and, when full, the hod tips to pour the sand into the hod of the builder immediately below – and so on to the base of the building, the sequence repeating until the store of sand runs out.

SAND-POWERED TOYS

Sand was once used to make simple toys move. It was made to flow downwards through a hopper, harnessing the power of gravity and causing a wheel to turn in exactly the same manner as a waterwheel is revolved. Ballbearings operated similarly. In fact neither method proved popular in post-war days, and few examples using these methods were produced. Probably the best example was the 1950s English-made "Merry Builders," from Codeg, which depended upon falling sand to animate its tinplate building workers.

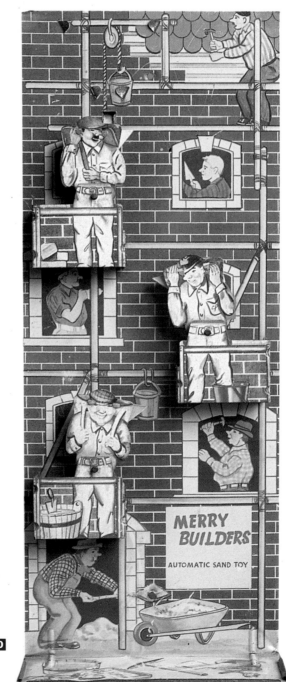

200

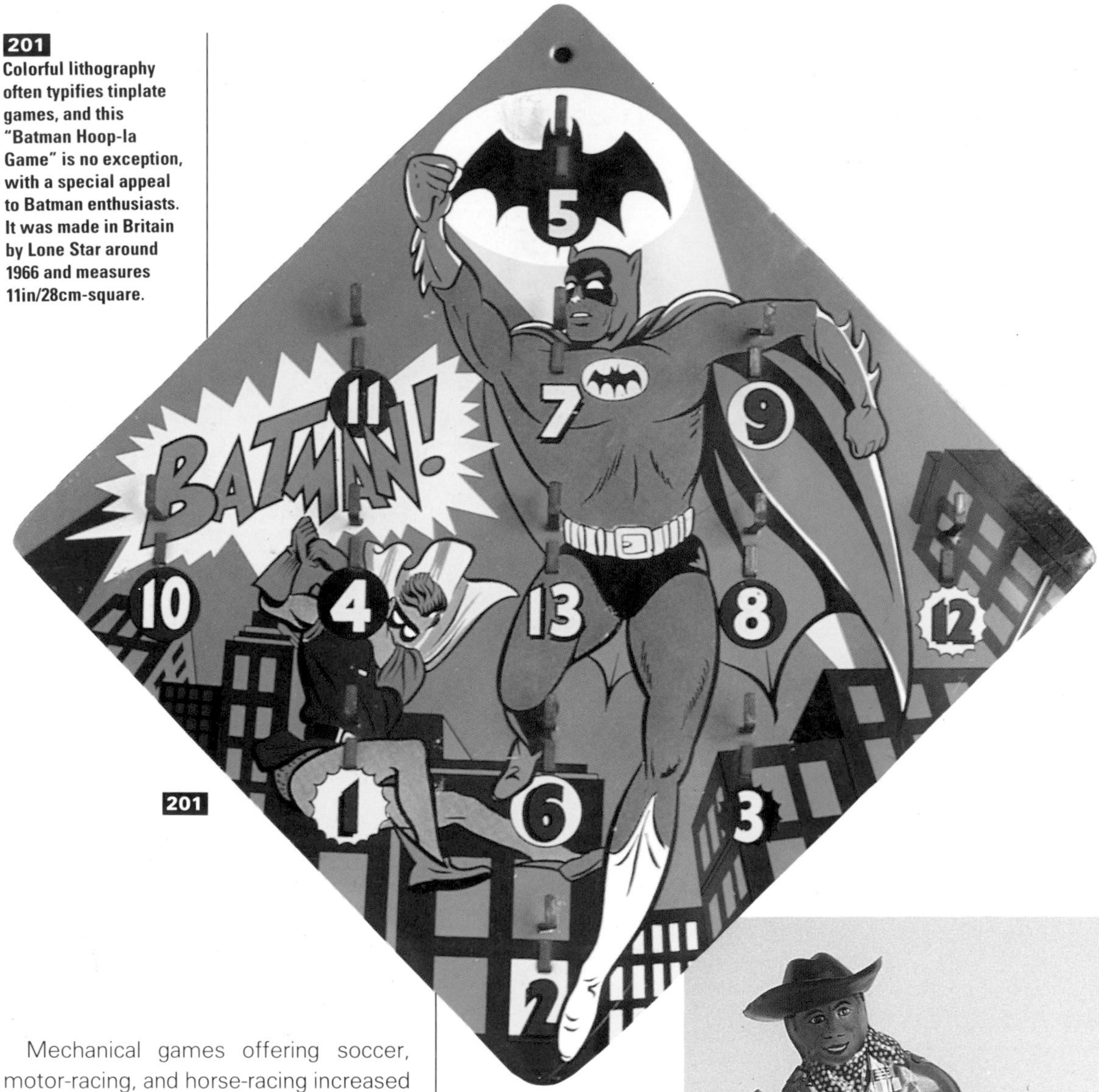

201
Colorful lithography often typifies tinplate games, and this "Batman Hoop-la Game" is no exception, with a special appeal to Batman enthusiasts. It was made in Britain by Lone Star around 1966 and measures 11in/28cm-square.

201

202
Pick up the pistol (made of plastic) and shoot at the tinplate cowboy. He can draw fast and shoot back, the pistol shots being reproduced by a hidden roll-cap firing mechanism within the toy. The exact maker is unknown, although the toy was made in the UK in the 1950s. The figure is 9in/23cm tall.

202

Mechanical games offering soccer, motor-racing, and horse-racing increased the thrill of competition on a small scale. They were produced with varying grades of skill, perhaps the best coming from West Germany. An example is the detailed Technofix soccer game which featured well-made tinplate figures. Shooting games imitated the style of the larger machines that once prevailed in coin-operated amusement arcades at seaside resorts and bars. They generally required the shooting down of a row of tinplate animal or human figures, using tinplate pistols firing small ball-bearings.

A number of magic lanterns were available in the shops — usually small, simple models designed to project slides or film strips. Some of these were attractively produced, but others were little more than flashlamps which projected a picture on to a hanging sheet or a plainly painted wall. These have never been in much demand by collectors, though again, the exceptions which proved the rule are those decorated with comic character figures – or which came with slides of any of these.

This "character" element also affects the popularity of such ordinary tinplate items as children's seaside sand-buckets, manufactured in many countries. Chad Valley issued several of these colorfully decorated items. Tinplate frog "clickers" and other small printed metal toys were made as stocking gifts or included in breakfast cereal boxes.

Tin TV screens contained winding panoramas, designed to give a primitive "moving picture" effect, flat tin figures, nicely decorated tin tea-sets, toy watches, and tin "Jack-in-the-Boxes" (with "Jack" usually being a molded plastic figure), schoolchildren's sheet-metal folding desks, and various musical instruments are all examples of colorful, often neglected, toys produced from the late 1940s to the end of the "Tinplate Age." One unusual and particularly interesting tinplate curiosity was a musical rattle – for want of a better description – produced as a commemorative novelty for the Coronation of Queen Elizabeth II. It carried a picture of the Queen-to-be, and

203

203

Nomura of Japan manufactured this 1950s curiosity – a tinplate gorilla acting as the target in a shooting game aptly named the "Roaring Gorilla Shooting Gallery." It comes complete with a fairly powerful tinplate cork-firing pistol. Take careful aim at the tinplate gorilla and if the cork hits the right place – a circular plate on its chest – the 9½in/24cm-tall creature shrieks in pain, raising his arms in the air, eyes flashing. This game is not easy to find complete; even when the box is available the pistol is often missing.

204

Tinplate guns were ever-popular children's toys, and those featuring a space or character theme are especially appealing to collectors. This highly collectible and rare tinplate battery-operated toy machine gun features Batman. It is 18in/46cm long and emits a chattering sound with flashing lights when the trigger is pressed.

204

suitable decoration. When twirled around the National Anthem tinkled from a simple internal musical mechanism!

Of course, children's cheap tinplate musical boxes, of the simple cylinder-shaped type which sounded "plink-plonk" notes when the crank handle at one end was turned, were commonly available. They have rarely been considered of great value – unless the illustrations were of sufficient interest to the collector. A little more expensive were the children's toy gramophones which appeared on the market from the 1950s onwards. These had clockwork motors and played acoustically, the sound being amplified by a simple, usually tin, horn. Chad Valley

made them, as did a number of German toymakers. They were amusing, though not hi-fi reproducers by any means.

Generally speaking, however intricate and ingenious many of these tinplate playthings – including toy sewing machines, typewriters, adding machines, and cash registers – are, few hold much interest for collectors. Usually such toys are bought up cheaply by people who have opened toy museums, to fill up their showcases.

Tin buildings will obviously be sought after by some collectors and they are not

205 206
"Clacker" toys are just one example of the numerous small, cheaply priced tin toys produced. These clackers were made by T Conn in the United States, probably in the 1950s, and are typically colorful in decoration and no doubt made enough noise to amuse their original young owners.

207

208
Batman and Robin figures decorate this small (1½in/4cm in diameter) spinning top from the 1960s. This example is 100 per cent tinplate, but later issues had a plastic base. The top's origin is unknown, although it was certainly a give-away toy.

207
The "Orbitoy" was a novelty plaything marketed by Dunbee-Combex in the 1960s. It is colorfully lithographed with an outer-space vista that enhances its collectibility. It resembles a large tinplate yo-yo and features a magnetic satellite which travels in orbit around the groove where the yo-yo string would be wound. It is 9½in/24cm in diameter.

easy to find, as not many were marketed. Toy record-players often appeal to gramophone enthusiasts, who like to add them to their collections – they appear to have a reasonable following, in any case. Again their decoration plays a big part in increasing their appeal. Since collecting is something of a fickle business, anything might happen, and it is possible that by the time this book appears in the shops, the pendulum may have swung in the opposite direction. Perhaps these lesser tin toys will have suddenly become highly desirable – who can tell what the future holds?

209

209

Tinplate clockwork toy gramophones were more popular in the 1930s, but the German firm of GAMA tried reintroducing them in the 1950s. They actually played, and usually came with one or two small 78 rpm records of the breakable variety – not ideal for handling by children. This one was known as the "Pixie Phone" and is 8½in/22cm long.

210

This tinplate typewriter, measuring 10in/25cm across, was produced by the British firm of Mettoy in the 1960s. Its typing action is simple, but reasonably effective. Toys such as these, including sewing machines and cash registers, are not highly collectible and are therefore less expensive to buy at present.

210

TOY MUSEUMS

All the following display old toys, although some may not feature post-war examples

COUNTRY	NAME	LOCATION
BELGIUM	MUSEE DU JOUET	BRUSSELS
	TOY MUSEUM	MECHELEN (MALINES)
CANADA	BAND COLLECTION	MTRCA, TORONTO
DENMARK	THE TOY MUSEUM	GAMST, JUTLAND
	TOY AND DOLL MUSEUM	'LEGOLAND', AARHUS
	TOY AND DOLL MUSEUM	COPENHAGEN
FRANCE	ATLANTRAIN MUSEUM	ST JUST-LUZAC, MARENNES
	MUSÉE DES ARTS DECORATIFS	THE LOUVRE, PARIS
	MUSÉE RAMBOLITRAIN	RAMBOUILLET
GERMANY	DEUTSCHES SPIELZEUGMUSEUM	SONNEBERG
	STATE TOY MUSEUM	NUREMBERG
REPUBLIC OF IRELAND	TOY & DOLL MUSEUM	DUBLIN
SWITZERLAND	MUSÉE D'ART ET D'HISTOIRE	NEUCHATEL
UNITED KINGDOM	ABBEY HOUSE MUSEUM	KIRSTALL, LEEDS, W YORKS
	COCKTHORPE HALL TOY MUSEUM	COCKTHORPE, WELLS, NORFOLK
	DOLL AND TOY MUSEUM	CHESTER
	THE INCREDIBLY FANTASTIC TOY MUSEUM	LINCOLN
	LONDON TOY MUSEUM	LONDON
	MUSEUM OF CHILDHOOD	RIBCHESTER, LANCS
	MUSEUM OF CHILDHOOD	HAWORTH, W YORKS
	MUSEUM OF CHILDHOOD	GLENDALE, ISLE OF SKYE
	MUSEUM OF CHILDHOOD	BEAUMARIS, ANGLESEY, WALES
	MUSEUM OF CHILDHOOD	BETHNAL GREEN, LONDON
	MUSEUM OF CHILDHOOD	EDINBURGH, SCOTLAND
	POLLOCK'S TOY MUSEUM	LONDON
	TOLSON MUSEUM	HUDDERSFIELD, W YORKS
	TOY AND DOLL MUSEUM	HEBDEN BRIDGE, W YORKS
	TOY AND TEDDY BEAR MUSEUM	LYTHAM ST ANNES, LANCS
	TOY AND TRAIN MUSEUM	FIELD'S DEPT STORE, SIDMOUTH, DEVON
	TOY COLLECTION	SUDBURY HALL, DERBY
	TOY COLLECTION	LYMPNE CASTLE, CANTERBURY, KENT
	TOY COLLECTION	THIRLSTANE CASTLE, LAUDER, SCOTLAND
	TOY MUSEUM	COCKERMOUTH, CUMBRIA
	VINA COOKE DOLL MUSEUM	CROMWELL, NOTTS
UNITED STATES	ANGEL'S ATTIC	SANTA MONICA, CA
	HISTORICAL SOCIETY MUSEUM	NEW YORK
	INTERNATIONAL TOY MUSEUM	SAN FRANCISCO, CA
	PLAYHOUSE MUSEUM	LAS CRUCES, NM
	SAMUEL'S COMIC TOY MUSEUM	ST LOUIS, MO
	SMITHSONIAN INSTITUTE	WASHINGTON DC
	THE MUSEUM OF CHILDHOOD	DOUGLASVILLE, PA
	TIME WAS VILLAGE MUSEUM	MENDOTA, IL
	TOY MUSEUM	ATLANTA, GA
	YORKTOWN MUSEUM	YORKTOWN HEIGHTS, NY
USSR	STATE MUSEUM	ZAGORSK

TOY COLLECTORS' FAIRS

COUNTRY	FAIR	TOWN
AUSTRALIA	ANTIQUE TOY & DOLL FAIR	PADDINGTON, SYDNEY
BELGIUM	TOY FAIR	MECHELEN (MALINES)
CANADA	TOY & MODEL FAIR	TORONTO
	TOY FAIR	WATERLOO, ONTARIO
DENMARK	TOY FAIR	COPENHAGEN
FRANCE	TOY & MODEL FAIR	LILLE
	TOY FAIR	MULHOUSE
	'TOYMANIA'	PARIS
	TOY SWAPMEET	RAMBOUILLET
	MODEL TOY BOURSE	ST OUEN L'AUMONE
GERMANY	TOY FAIR	BERLIN
	TOY COLLECTORS' FAIR	BIELEFELD
	DOLL & OLD TOY FAIR	COLOGNE
	TRAIN & TOY FAIR	GRÜNSTADT
	DOLLS & OLD TOYS FAIR	KIEL
	TOY AND TRAIN MARKET	PLANEGG. NR MUNICH
	TRAIN & MODEL CAR MARKET	PLANKSTADT
	TOY FAIR	RECHLINGHAUSEN
	DOLLS & OLD TOYS FAIR	TRAVEMÜNDE
	TOY & DOLL FAIR	WIESBADEN
	TOY & TRAIN MARKET	WUPPERTAL
ITALY	MODEL CAR & ANTIQUE TOY FAIR	PIACENZA
THE NETHERLANDS	TRAIN COLLECTORS' FAIR	AMERSFOORT
	TOY MARKET	AMSTERDAM
	TOY FAIR	BERGEN-OP-ZOOM
	TOY FAIR	DEVENTER
	MODEL RAILWAY FAIR	HAARLEM
	TRAIN MARKET	HEERLEN
NEW ZEALAND	TOY FAIR	AUCKLAND
SOUTH AFRICA	TOY COLLECTORS' FAIR	PRETORIA
SWEDEN	TOY COLLECTORS' FAIR	HELSINGBORG
	TOY FAIR	STOCKHOLM
UNITED KINGDOM	GRAMPIAN TOY FAIR	ABERDEEN, SCOTLAND
	COLLECTORS' TOY FAIR	BALLYMENA, N IRELAND
	TOY FAIR	BRIDGNORTH, SHROPS
	TOY SWAPMEET	BRISTOL, AVON
	TOY COLLECTORS' FAIR	BUXTON, DERBYS
	COLLECTORS' TOY FAIR	CARLISLE, CUMBRIA
	GIANT TOY FAIR	CASTLE DONINGTON, LEICS
	MOVIE & SCI-FI FAIR	CHESHUNT, HERTS
	TOY & TRAIN SWAPMEET	CHESTER
	TOY COLLECTORS' FAIR	COVENTRY, W MIDS
	TOY COLLECTORS' FAIR	CRAWLEY, SUSSEX
	TAYSIDE TOY FAIR	DUNDEE, SCOTLAND
	TOY & MODEL FAIR	FARNHAM, SURREY
	SCI-FI FAIR	FELTHAM, LONDON
	TRAIN & TOY FAIR	GAINSBOROUGH, LINCS
	TOY & MODEL FAIR	GLASGOW, SCOTLAND
	TOY & TRAIN FAIR	GLOUCESTER
	TOY SWAPMEET	LEEDS, W YORKS
	SCI-FI & FANTASY FAIR	LEICESTER
	TOY & TRAIN FAIR	LINCOLN
	TRAIN & TOY FAIR	LIVERPOOL
	TOY SWAPMEET	LUTON, BEDS

COUNTRY	FAIR	TOWN
UNITED KINGDOM	TOY COLLECTORS' FAIR	MALVERN, HEREF & WORCS
	TOY FAIR	MANCHESTER
	TOYFAIR & SWAPMEET	NEWTOWNABBEY, N IRELAND
	TOY & TRAIN FAIR	NOTTINGHAM
	TOY SWAPMEET	PAIGNTON, DEVON
	TOY FAIR	RUGBY, WARKS
	TOY EXTRAVAGANZA	SANDOWN PARK, LONDON
	WINDSOR SWAPMEET	SLOUGH, BERKS
	TOY FAIR	SOUTHAMPTON, HANTS
	TRAIN & TOY SALE	STRATFORD-UPON-AVON, WARKS
	TRAIN & TOY FAIR	WARRINGTON, CHESHIRE
	COLLECTORS' TOY FAIR	WEST CROYDON, LONDON
	TOY & MODEL FAIR	YORK, BEDS
UNITED STATES	TOY SHOW	ALBANY, NY
	SUPER NOVA TOY SHOW	ALEXANDRIA, VA
	TOY & ANTIQUE SHOW	BELLEVUE, WA
	FARM TOY SHOW	BILLINGS, MT
	TOY & HOBBY SHOW	BOONE, NC
	TOY SHOW & SALE	BUENA PARK, CA
	COLLECTIBLES SHOW	DALLAS, TX
	ANTIQUE TOY SHOW	DAYTON, OH
	DISNEY COLLECTORS' SHOW	DEDHAM, MA
	GREENBERG'S TRAIN & TOY SHOW	EDISON, NJ
	TOY FAIR	EPHRATA, PA
	ANTIQUE TOY & TRAIN SHOW	FORT WAYNE, IN
	COLLECTORS' SHOW	GLENDALE, CA
	S E TOY SHOW	GREENVILLE, SC
	ANTIQUE TOY & TRAIN SHOW	INDIANAPOLIS, IN
	TOY CONVENTION	KENNEDY AIRPORT, NY
	TOY FAIR	LONG BEACH, CA
	ANTIQUE TOY SHOW	LEXINGTON, KY
	WEST-LA TOY SHOW	LOS ANGELES, CA
	TOY CONVENTION	NEWARK, NJ
	TOY & COLLECTIBLES SHOW	NEW HOPE, PA
	TOY SWAPMEET	NORTHBROOK, IL
	TOY SHOW	OMAHA, NE
	TOY SHOW	PASADENA, CA
	TOY & TRAIN MEET	PENNDEL, PA
	GREENBERG'S TRAIN & TOY SHOW	PHILADELPHIA, PA
	TOY & TRAIN MEET	PHILLIPSBURG, NJ
	TOY ROUND-UP	PHOENIX, AZ
	TOY & HOBBY SHOW	RALEIGH, NC
	GREENBERG'S TRAIN & TOY SHOW	RICHMOND, VA
	ANNUAL TOY SHOW	ROGERSVILLE, MO
	ANTIQUE & COLLECTIBLES SHOW	SAN FRANCISCO, CA
	FARM TOY SHOW	SAUK CENTRE, MN
	MID-AMERICAN TOY SHOW	ST LOUIS, MO
	NY FARM TOY SHOW	SYRACUSE, NY
	GREENBERG'S GREAT TOY SHOW	TOWSON, MD
	TOY & TRAIN MEET	WALLINGFORD, CT
	TOY & TRAIN SHOW	WARRINGTON, PA
	TOY SHOW	WHEATON, IL
	MODEL CAR SWAPMEET	WORTH, IL

An alphabetical cross-referenced listing of company names and their trademarks. Where trademarks are virtually identical to the company names, they have not been cross-referenced.

NAME/'TRADEMARK'	TOWN	COUNTRY	'TRADEMARK'/NAME
'A1'			SEE ASAKUSA
'AHI'			SEE AOSHIN
ALADDIN INDUSTRIES	NASHVILLE, TN	USA	'ALADDIN'
ALEMANNI	MILAN	ITALY	'LAC'
ALPS SHOJI LTD	TOKYO	JAPAN	'ALPS' OVER MOUNTAIN LOGO
AMBROSI	ROME	ITALY	'AMBROSI'
AOSHIN	TOKYO	JAPAN	'ASC'; 'AHI'
ARNOLD	NUREMBERG	GERMANY	'ARNOLD' IN TRIANGLE LOGO
ARTLAY MFG CO	SYDNEY	AUSTRALIA	'BOOMAROO'
ASAHI TOY CO	TOKYO	JAPAN	'ASAHI' ON 'A'
ASAKUSA TOYS LTD	TOKYO	JAPAN	'A1'
'ASC'			SEE AOSHIN
'ATOM'			SEE TADA
'B' IN KEY LOGO			SEE BILLER
BALDWIN MFG CO	BROOKLYN, NY	USA	
BANDAI CO LTD	TOKYO	JAPAN	'BC' MONOGRAM
BASSETT-LOWKE LTD	NORTHAMPTON	UK	'LOWCO'
'BC' MONOGRAM			SEE BANDAI
BELL COMPANY	MILAN	ITALY	'BELL'
'BETAL'			SEE GLASMAN
BILIKEN	TOKYO	JAPAN	'BILIKEN'
BILLER	NUREMBERG	GERMANY	'B' IN KEY LOGO
BING, GEBRÜDER	NUREMBERG	GERMANY	'BW' MOTIF
BLACK CAT LOGO			SEE CIEN GE TOYS
BLOMER & SCHÜLER	NUREMBERG	GERMANY	'B&S' & ELEPHANT LOGO
BOLZ, LAURENZ	ZIRNDORF	GERMANY	'LBZ'
BONNET, VICTOR	PARIS	FRANCE	'VEBE'
'BOOMAROO'			SEE ARTLAY
BOWMAN MODELS	DEREHAM	UK	'BOWMAN' & RED INDIAN LOGO
BRANDSTÄTTER	ZIRNDORF	GERMANY	'GEOBRA'
BRIMTOY LTD	LONDON	UK	NELSON'S COLUMN LOGO
'B&S' & ELEPHANT LOGO			SEE BLOMER & SCHÜLER
BUB, KARL	NUREMBERG	GERMANY	'KB'; 'KBN'
BUCHERER & CO	DIEPOLDSAU	SWITZERLAND	'BUCO'
'BUCO'			SEE BUCHERER
BÜHLER	NUREMBERG	GERMANY	FIR TREE LOGO
BULLMARK TOYS	TOKYO	JAPAN	'BULLMARK'
'BW'			SEE BING, GEBRÜDER
CAMBRIAN CO	PORT TALBOT	UK	'CAMTOY'
'CAMTOY'			SEE CAMBRIAN
CENTOLA	BOLOGNA	ITALY	'FCR'
CHAD VALLEY	BIRMINGHAM	UK	'CHAD VALLEY'
CHEIN	NEW JERSEY	USA	'CHEIN'
CIEN GE TOYS		TAIWAN	BLACK CAT LOGO
'CKO'			SEE KELLERMANN
'CODEG'			SEE COWAN DE GROOT
'COMBEX'			SEE DUNBEE-COMBEX
COWAN DE GROOT	LONDON	UK	'CODEG'
'CR'			SEE ROSSIGNOL
CRAGSTAN	NEW YORK	USA	'CRAGSTAN'
DAISY MFG CO	ROGERS, AR	USA	'DAISY'
DAIYA	TOKYO	JAPAN	'DAIYA'

NAME/'TRADEMARK'	TOWN	COUNTRY	'TRADEMARK'/NAME
DISTLER	NUREMBERG	GERMANY	'JDN' IN WORLD GLOBE LOGO
'DUBLO'			SEE MECCANO
DUNBEE-COMBEX	LONDON	UK	'COMBEX'
DUNBEE-COMBEX-MARX	LONDON	UK	'MARX'
'DUX'			SEE MARKES
'E' & BELL LOGO			SEE LEHMANN
EINFALT, GEBRÜDER	NUREMBERG	GERMANY	'TECHNOFIX'
'ERACTOR'			SEE GILBERT
'FAIRYLITE'			SEE GRAHAM BROS
'FCR'			SEE CENTOLA
FERRARI S	CASALPUSTERLENGO	ITALY	'FSC'
FIR TREE LOGO			SEE BÜHLER
FISCHER, GEORG	NUREMBERG	GERMANY	'GF' MONOGRAM
FLARE CORP	NEW YORK	USA	'FLARE'
FLEISCHMANN, J	NUREMBERG	GERMANY	'GFN'
FLIM	BUDAPEST	HUNGARY	'FLIM'
FOURNEREAU	SEINE-ET-OISE	FRANCE	'JFJ'
'FSC'			SEE FERRARI
FUCHS & CO	NUREMBERG	GERMANY	'FUCHS' & FOXHEAD LOGO
'GAMA'			SEE MANGOLD
'GEOBRA'			SEE BRANDSTÄTTER
'GESCHA'			SEE SCHMID, GEBRÜDER
'GF' MONOGRAM			SEE FISCHER, GEORG
'GFN'			SEE FLEISCHMANN, J
GILBERT CO	CHICAGO, IL	USA	'ERACTOR'
'GKN' IN TRIANGLE LOGO			SEE KÖHLER
GLASMAN LTD	LONDON	UK	'BETAL'
'GM & CIE'			SEE MÄRKLIN
'GOSO'			SEE GÖTZ & SOHN
GÖTZ & SOHN	FÜRTH	GERMANY	'GOSO'
GRAHAM BROS	LONDON	UK	'FAIRYLITE'
GÜNTHERMANN	NUREMBERG	GERMANY	'SG'
GUTMANN	PARIS	FRANCE	'MEMO'
'HAJI'			SEE MANSEI
HÖFFLER	FÜRTH	GERMANY	'JH' IN CLOVERLEAF LOGO
HORIKAWA TOYS	TOKYO	JAPAN	'SH' IN DIAMOND LOGO
'HORNBY'			SEE MECCANO
'HUKI'			SEE KIENBERGER
'HWN'			SEE WIMMER
'ICG'			SEE INCO-GIOCHI
ICHIKO KOGYO CO	TOKYO	JAPAN	'PU'
INCO-GIOCHI	TURIN	ITALY	'ICG'
INGAP	PADUA	ITALY	'INGAP'
INGAT	TURIN	ITALY	LION'S HEAD LOGO
'INTERKOZMOSZ'			SEE LEMAVAR GYAR
'JDN' IN WORLD GLOBE LOGO			SEE DISTLER
JEP (JOUETS DE PARIS)	PARIS	FRANCE	'JEP'
'JFJ'			SEE FOURNEREAU
'JH' IN CLOVERLEAF LOGO			SEE HOFFLER
'JNF'			SEE NEUHIERL, JOHANN
JOUSTRA	STRASBOURG	FRANCE	'JOUSTRA'
JYE	IBI	SPAIN	'JYE'

NAME/'TRADEMARK'	TOWN	COUNTRY	'TRADEMARK'/NAME
KANTO TOYS	TOKYO	JAPAN	'KO'
'KB'			SEE BUB, KARL
'KBN'			SEE BUB, KARL
KELLERMANN & CO	NUREMBERG	GERMANY	'CKO'
'KI-CO'			SEE KIENBERGER
KIENBERGER	NUREMBERG	GERMANY	'HUKI'; 'KI-CO'
'KO'			SEE KANTO
KÖHLER	NUREMBERG	GERMANY	'GKN' IN TRIANGLE LOGO
'LAC'			SEE ALEMANNI
'LBZ'			SEE BOLZ, LAURENZ
LEHMANN	NUREMBERG	GERMANY	'E' IN BELL LOGO
LEMAVAR GYAR		HUNGARY	'INTERKOZMOSZ'
LENIN MEMORIAL FACTORY	MOSCOW	USSR	'V' INVERTED
LINEMAR TOYS	TOKYO	JAPAN	'LINEMAR'
LINES BROS LTD	LONDON	UK	'TRI-ANG'; 'MINIC'
LION'S HEAD LOGO			SEE INGAT
LIONEL	NEW YORK	USA	'LIONEL'
LONE STAR	LONDON	UK	'LONE STAR'
LOVELY TOYS INC	DELHI	INDIA	'LTI'
'LOWCO'			SEE BASSETT-LOWKE
'LTI'			SEE LOVELY TOYS – AKA BEAUTY TOYS; TINA
MAMOD LTD	ASCOT	UK	'MAMOD'
MANGOLD	FÜRTH	GERMANY	'GAMA'; 'SCHUCO'
MANSEI TOY CO	TOKYO	JAPAN	'HAJI'
MAR TOYS	SWANSEA	UK	'MAR TOYS' IN CIRCLE LOGO
MARCHESINI, L	BOLOGNA	ITALY	'MARCHESINI'
MARKES & CO	LÜDENSCHEID	GERMANY	'DUX'
MÄRKLIN	GÖPPINGEN	GERMANY	'GM & CIE'
MARUSAN TOYS	TOKYO	JAPAN	'SAN'
MARX & CO LTD	NEW YORK	USA	'MARX'
MARX & CO LTD	SWANSEA	UK	'MARX'
MASUDAYA			AKA MASUTOKU
MASUTOKU TOY FACTORY	TOKYO	JAPAN	'MT' MONOGRAM
MASUYA TOYS			AKA MASUTOKU
MECCANO	LIVERPOOL	UK	'HORNBY'; 'DUBLO'
MEGO CORP	TOKYO	JAPAN	'MEGO'
'MEMO'			SEE GUTMANN
METTOY	LONDON	UK	'METTOY'
'MINIC'			SEE 'TRI-ANG'; LINES BROS
MINIMODELS LTD	LONDON	UK	'STARTEX'
MODERN TOYS			AKA MASUTOKU
'MT' MONOGRAM			SEE MASUTOKU
MULLER, F W	BERLIN	GERMANY	'REGINA'
NELSON'S COLUMN LOGO			SEE BRIMTOY
NEUHIERL, JOHANN, GmbH	FÜRTH	GERMANY	'JNF'
NIEDERMEIER, PHILLIP	NUREMBERG	GERMANY	'PN'
NOMURA TOYS	TOKYO	JAPAN	'TN'
NUREMBERG TIN TOYS	NUREMBERG	GERMANY	
OMAS	TURIN	ITALY	'OMAS'
PAYA	ALICANTE	SPAIN	'PAYA'
PLAYTHING CO	TOKYO	JAPAN	'PLAYTHING'
'PN'			SEE NIEDERMEIER, PHILLIP
PRESTYN TOYS LTD	LONDON	UK	'PRESTYN'
'PU'			SEE ICHIKO

NAME/'TRADEMARK'	TOWN	COUNTRY	'TRADEMARK'/NAME
RABBIT HEAD LOGO			SEE USAGIYA
'REGINA'			SEE MULLER, F W
RICO	IBI	SPAIN	'RICO'
ROCK VALLEY TOYS	TOKYO	JAPAN	'VIA'
ROMA		SPAIN	
ROSSIGNOL	PARIS	FRANCE	'CR'
RSA	ALICANTE	SPAIN	'RSA'
'SAN'			SEE MARUSAN
SCHMID, GEBRÜDER	ROCKENHOF	GERMANY	'GESCHA'
SCHREYER & CO	NUREMBERG	GERMANY	'SCHUCO'
SCHRODER & CO	LÜDENSCHEID	GERMANY	'WILESCO'
'SCHUCO'			SEE MANGOLD; SCHREYER
'SEL' MONOGRAM			SEE SIGNALLING EQUIPMENT LTD
SIGNALLING EQUIPMENT LTD	LONDON	UK	'SEL'
'SG'			SEE GÜNTHERMANN
'SH' IN DIAMOND LOGO			SEE HORIKAWA
'STARTEX'			SEE MINIMODELS
STRONLITE	TOKYO	JAPAN	'STRONLITE'
SUTCLIFFE LTD	HORSFORTH	UK	'SUTCLIFFE'
TADA	TOKYO	JAPAN	'ATOM'
TAIYO KOGYO	TOKYO	JAPAN	'TAIYO'
'TECHNOFIX'			SEE EINFALT
TIPP & CO	NUREMBERG	GERMANY	'TIPPCO'
'TIPPCO'			SEE TIPP
'TN'			SEE NOMURA
TONKA CO	TOKYO	JAPAN	'TONKA'
TOPLAY	TOKYO	JAPAN	'TPS'
'TPS'			SEE TOPLAY
'TRI-ANG'			SEE LINES BROS
TUCHER & WALTHER	NUREMBERG	GERMANY	
UNIQUE ART	NEWARK, NJ	USA	'UNIQUE ART'
USAGIYA	TOKYO	JAPAN	RABBIT HEAD LOGO
'V' INVERTED			SEE LENIN
VEB	BRANDENBURG	GERMANY	'VEB'
'VEBE'			SEE BONNET, VICTOR
'VIA'			SEE ROCK VALLEY TOYS
VICTORY INDUSTRIES	LONDON	UK	'VICTORY'
WACO CO	TOKYO	JAPAN	'WACO'
WELLS-BRIMTOY	LONDON	UK	'WELLS'
WESTERN STAMPING CO	DETROIT	USA	
'WILESCO'			SEE SCHRODER
'WILLOW'			SEE WILSON
WILSON BROS LTD	MELBOURNE	AUSTRALIA	'WILLOW'
WIMMER	NUREMBERG	GERMANY	'HWN'
WÜCO			SEE FRITZ WÜNNERLEIN
WÜNNERLEIN, FRITZ, & CO	ZIRNDORF	GERMANY	'WÜCO'
WYANDOTTE MFG CO	WYANDOTTE, MI	USA	
WYN PRODUCTS PTY LTD	EAST SYDNEY	AUSTRALIA	'WYN-TOY'
'Y' IN FLOWER LOGO			SEE YONEZAWA
YAMAMURA & CO	KOBE	JAPAN	'YAMAMURA'
YANOMAN TOYS	TOKYO	JAPAN	'YM'
'YM'			SEE YANOMAN TOYS
'YONE'			SEE YONEYA
YONEYA TOYS CO	TOKYO	JAPAN	'YONE'
YONEZAWA CO	TOKYO	JAPAN	'Y' IN FLOWER LOGO

BIBLIOGRAPHY

TITLE	AUTHOR	PUBLISHED	DATE
AMERICAN COLLECTIBLES	CHRISTOPHER PEARCE	NEW YORK, USA	1990
ANTIQUE DOLLS & TOYS	ROMY ROEDER	AUSTRALIA	1985
ART OF THE TIN TOY	DAVID PRESSLAND	LONDON, UK	1976
AUTO-GIOCATTOLO ITALIANE	PAOLO RAMPINI	MILAN, ITALY	1986
BATTERY TOYS	BRIAN MORAN	USA	1984
BRITISH TIN TOYS	MARGUERITE FAWDRY	LONDON, UK	1990
CHARACTER TOYS	DAVID LONGEST	PADUCAH, USA	1987
CHILDREN'S TOYS THROUGHOUT THE AGES	LESLIE DAIKEN	LONDON, UK	1963
COLLECTING TOYS	WC KETCHUM, JR	TUCSON, USA	1985
COLLECTING TIN TOYS	JACK TEMPEST	LONDON, UK	1987
COLLECTING THE TIN TOY CAR	DALE KELLEY	CHICAGO, USA	1984
COLLECTORS' GUIDE TO MODEL RAILWAYS	J JOYCE	WATFORD, UK	1977
DIE ANDEREN NURNBERGER (8 VOLS)	C BAECKER & D HAAS	FRANKFURT, GERMANY	1973
ENCYCLOPEDIA OF METAL TOYS	R O'NEILL	LONDON, UK	1988
ENCYCLOPEDIA OF TOY CARS	PAOLO RAMPINI	MILAN, ITALY	1984
ENCYCLOPEDIA OF 1/43 MODEL CARS	PAOLO RAMPINI	MILAN, ITALY	1990
ENGLISH DOLLS & TOYS	K & M FAWDRY	LONDON, UK	1979
GREAT BOOK OF CORGI	M R VAN CLEEMPUT	LONDON, UK	1989
HORNY DUBLO POST-WAR	TONY OAKES	NANTWICH, UK	1990
HORNBY DUBLO TRAINS	MICHAEL FOSTER	LONDON, UK	1988
JEP, JOUET DE PARIS – 1902–1968	CLIVE LAMMING	PARIS, FRANCE	1988
LEXICON BLECHSPIELZEUG	KURT HARRER	GERMANY	1982
MECHANICAL TIN TOYS	ARNO WELTENS	POOLE, UK	1977
MECHANICAL TOYS	C BARTHOLOMEW	FELTHAM, UK	1979
METAL TOYS	RICHARD O'NEILL	LONDON, UK	1984
MINIC	S RICHARDSON	WINDSOR, UK	1981
MODEL & MINIATURE RAILWAYS	WHITEHOUSE & ADAMS	LONDON, UK	1976
MOTOS-JOUETS	F MARCHAND	PARIS, FRANCE	1985
PENNY BANK BOOK	ANDY & SUSAN MOORE	EXTON, USA	1984
PLAYTHINGS PAST	BETTY CADBURY	LONDON, UK	1976
PRICE GUIDE TO METAL TOYS	GARDINER & MORRIS	WOODBRIDGE, UK	1980
RECENT LOCOMOTIVES	P E RANDALL	LONDON, UK	1970
ROBOT	PIERRE BOOGAERTS	PARIS, FRANCE	1978
SCHUCO SAMMLER-KATALOG	BULDT & LIEHM	DORTMUND, GERMANY	1988
THE TOY COLLECTOR	LOUIS HERTZ	NEW YORK, USA	1967
THE WORLD OF TOYS	ROBERT CULFF	LONDON, UK	1969
TIN TOY DREAMS	T KITAHARA	TOKYO, JAPAN	1985
TIN TOYS, 1945–1975	MICHAEL BUHLER	LONDON, UK	1978
TOY BOATS	BASIL HARLEY	PRINCES RISBOROUGH, UK	1987
TOY BOATS, 1870–1955	MILET & FORBES	NEW YORK, USA	1979
TOY CARS	GARDINER & O'NEILL	LONDON, UK	1985
TOYS	McGIMPSEY & ORR	LONDON, UK	1990
TOYS	PATRICK MURRAY	LONDON, UK	1968
TOYSHOP STEAM	BASIL HARLEY	WATFORD, UK	1978
WORLD OF TOYS	LESLIE DAIKEN	LONDON, UK	1963

Price Guide

Harry L. Rinker

© *Rinker Enterprises 1991*

Postwar tin toys are one of the hottest segments in the American toy market. The generation that played with them is suffering a serious case of nostalgia. They have advanced far enough in their careers to provide them with ample discretionary income so that they can buy back their childhood, which, on the whole, is still affordable.

However, American collectors are finding that they are not alone in the pursuit of their childhood treasures. Foreign buyers, notably collectors from Europe and Japan, have besieged American flea markets, toy shows, shops, malls, and auctions. The market is truly international; and, America is the great mother lode.

Because collecting postwar tin toys is relatively new, pricing is extremely volatile. A number of dealers are manipulating segments of the market with the goal to drive prices continually upward. The robot market is an excellent example. Collectors and dealers alike are speculating heavily across the entire spectrum of postwar tin toys. A $50.00 toy might be $100.00 six months from now only to fall back to $50.00 in two to three years as market crazes shift. Postwar tin toys are not the place for individuals with either weak hearts or pocket books.

Beginning collectors are advised to spend several months studying the market before making their initial purchases. Comparative shopping makes a great deal of sense. Remember these toys were made in large quantities, often in the millions. Prices for the same toy can differ as much as two to four hundred percent at the same flea market or show.

Condition is critical when buying postwar tin toys. If a toy shows signs of heavy use or is damaged in any fashion, DO NOT BUY IT. Set extremely tough con-

No	Description	Maker	Provenance	Date	Very Good	Excellent
INTRODUCTION						
1	Clockwork clown and dog	Unknown	UK	1950s-1960s	$135	$185
2	Porsche sports car	Rico	Spain	1960s	$50	$85
3	Mechanical 'Esso' tiger	Marx	USA	1960s	$125	$200
4	'Mystery Car'	Neuhierl	Germany	1960s	$125	$200
5	Somersaulting monkey	Unknown	Germany	1950s	$50	$90
6	Clockwork walking horse and rider	Unknown	Japan	1940s-1950s	$75	$125
7	Clockwork mounted soldier and cannon	Unknown	Japan	1940s-1950s	$75	$125
8	'Grand Prix Racer'; battery-powered	Yonezawa	Japan	1950s	$150	$250
9	'Hello Car'; battery-powered	Nomura	Japan	1950s	$200	$275
10	Jumpin' jeep	Marx	USA	1947	$120	$160
11	G.I. Joe and his Jouncing jeep	Unique Art Mfg Co	USA	1950s	$125	$200
12	US Army truck	Marx	USA	1950s	$60	$80
13	'Passenger Plane'; friction-drive	Unknown	China	Current	—	
14	'MS 134' clockwork space vehicle	Unknown	Japan	1970s-1980s	$50	$75
COLLECTING POST-WAR TIN TOYS						
15	Mechanical tractor	Mettoy	UK	1950s	$75	$125
16	'Magic Bulldozer'; battery-powered	Nomura	Japan	1950s	$100	$150
17	'Dapper Dan'; inertia-powered car	Kanto	Japan	1960s	$100	$150
18	Clockwork Batman figure	Biliken	Japan	Current	$75	$100
19	Batmobile	Yanoman	Japan	1960s	$750	$900
20	Batmobile; remote-controlled	Aoshin	Japan	1966	$450	$650
21	Batmobile; friction-drive	Aoshin	Japan	1966	$250	$325
22	Batmobile; battery-powered	Aoshin	Japan	1972	$325	$400
23	Batman automobile license plates	—	Hong Kong	1960s	$25	$45
24	Batplane; friction-drive	Unknown	Argentina	1950s	$600	$800
25	Batmobile; battery-operated	Aoshin	Japan	1966	$400	$600
26	Batmobile; battery-operated	—	Taiwan	1970s-1980s	$100	$150
27	Batmobile; battery-powered	Cien Ge Toys	Taiwan	1970s-1980s	$90	$140
28	Cycling boy with dog	Unknown	Japan	1950s	$45	$75
29	'Coney Island Scooter' bumper car	Kanto	Japan	1962	$80	$130
30	'Electromatic 7600' Jaguar car	Distler	Germany	1950s	$100	$150
31	Futuristic monorail toy; battery-powered	Nomura	Japan	1950s	$600	$850
32	Clockwork circus carousel	JML	France	1960s-1970s	$300	$450
33	'Crazy Jeep'; clockwork	Graham Bros	UK	1950	$125	$200
34	Boy and hippo; clockwork	Toplay	Japan	1950s-1960s	$350	$500
35	Clockwork marching soldier	Toplay	Japan	1960s-1970s	$35	$60
TINPLATE FIGURES						
36	Clockwork monkey and motorcycle	GAMA	Germany	1950s	$175	$250
37	'Candy Dog'; clockwork	Unknown	Japan	1950s	$45	$65
38	'Lazybones – the Sleeping Puppy'; clockwork	Alps Shoji	Japan	1950s	$85	$140
39	Basketball-playing monkey; clockwork	Toplay	Japan	1950s	$125	$200
40	Boy reading a book	Unknown	Japan	1950s	$85	$140
41	Bear reading a book	Unknown	Japan	1950s	$65	$100
42	Acrobatic monkeys	Unknown	Germany	1950s (Large)	$100	$150
				(Small)	$90	$135
43	Hungry rabbit; clockwork	Unknown	Japan	1960s	$45	$65
44	Acrobatic monkey	Toplay	Japan	1950s	$85	$140
45	Clockwork bear climbing ladder	Unknown	UK	1950s-1960s	$75	$130
46	'Animal Barber Shop'; clockwork	Toplay	Japan	1950s	$300	$400
47	'Violin Clown'; clockwork	Unknown	Japan	1950s	$225	$300
48	'Hobo Clown'; clockwork	Linemar	Japan	1950s	$300	$425
49	'Circus Boy'; clockwork	Nomura	Japan	1950s	$200	$260
50	Clown and performing dog	Toplay	Japan	1950s	$60	$100
51	Clown climbing pole; clockwork	Unknown	UK	1950s	$50	$90
52	'Good Time Charlie'; clockwork clown	Alps Shoji	Japan	1950s	$135	$190
53	'Bozo the Clown'; clockwork drummer	Alps Shoji	Japan	1950s	$90	$140
54	'Inverted Clown'; clockwork	Wells-Brimtoy	UK	1950s	$100	$150
55	'Jumbo' clockwork walking elephant	Lesney	UK	1950s	$95	$150
56	Clown and motor cycle; clockwork	Kanto	Japan	1950s	$100	$150
57	'Drummer Boy'; clockwork	Marx	USA	1950s-1960s	$125	$175
58	'Trumpet Player'; clockwork	Nomura	Japan	1950s-1960s	$75	$125
59	'Talking Parrot'	Asakusa	Japan	1950s-1960s	$75	$130
60	'Slugger Champions'; clockwork	Biller	Germany	1950s	$130	$200
61	'Animal House'; clockwork	Toplay	Japan	1950s	$175	$225
62	Battery-operated butterfly	Alps Shoji	Japan	1950s	$125	$175
63	Clockwork peacock	Blomer & Schüler	Germany	1950s	$150	$225
64	Clockwork turkey	Blomer & Schüler	Germany	1950s	$90	$150
65	Clockwork bird	Nomura	Japan	1960s	$40	$65
66	Trade catalog	Nomura	Japan	1950s	—	
67	'Charlie Weaver'; battery-powered	Nomura	Japan	1950s	$65	$85
68	'The Bartender'; clockwork	Nomura	Japan	1950s	$50	$75
69	'The Happy Miner'; remote-controlled	Ashai	Japan	1960s	$75	$110
70	'Strutting Sam'; battery powered	Unknown	Japan	1950s	$200	$275

71	'Tri-cycling Clown'; battery-powered	MT	Japan	1960s	$110	$160
72	'Sam the Shaving Man'; battery-powered	Plaything	Japan	1950s	$150	$200
73	'Circus Lion'; battery-powered	Rock Valley	Japan	1950s	$200	$275
74	'Smokey Bear'; battery-powered	Marusan	Japan	1950s	$125	$150
75	'Peppermint Twist'; battery-powered	Mego	Japan	1960s	$100	$150
76	'Accordion clown'; battery-powered	Rock Valley	Japan	1950s	$200	$275

CHARACTER TOYS

77	'Mickey Mouse Xylophone'; clockwork	Linemar	Japan	1950s	$600	$800
78	Clockwork Donald Duck	Schuco	Germany	1950s	$225	$275
79	'Mickey Mouse & Donald Duck Fire Engine'	Masudaya	Japan	1970s	$225	$300
80	'Popeye on Tricycle'; clockwork	Linemar	Japan	1950s	$800	$1,100
81	'Popeye Skater'; clockwork	Linemar	Japan	1950s	$750	$950
82	James Bond-style Aston-Martin car	Unknown	Japan	1960s	$125	$175
83	'Yeti'; clockwork	Unknown	Japan	1950s	$130	$175
84	Superman battling with tank; battery-powered	Linemar	Japan	1940s-1950s	$350	$500
85	'Godzilla'; battery-powered	Bullmark	Japan	1960s	$275	$375
86	Charlie MacCarthy driving clockwork jeep	Marx	USA	1940s-1950s	$400	$600

TINPLATE MOTOR VEHICLES

87	Car	Chad Valley	UK	1940s-1950s	$175	$225
88	'Magic Optomat' Mercedes 220S; clockwork	Kienberger	Germany	1950s-1960s	$160	$200
89	Clockwork car with spring-open hood and door	Joustra	France	1950s	$80	$125
90	Clockwork car; performs Y-turn	Joustra	France	1950s	$75	$110
91	Battery- and coin-operated car	Daiya	Japan	1970s	$60	$85
92	Friction-drive armored car/moneybox	Horikawa	Japan	1950s	$75	$100
93	'Auto Obstacle' clockwork car	Joustra	France	1950s	$75	$110
94	American station wagon; clockwork	Marchesini	Italy	1950s	$250	$325
95	'Highway Patrol Car'; battery-powered	Daiya	Japan	1970s	$65	$85
96	'Fire Department Fire Chief' car; friction-drive	Unknown	Japan	1950s-1960s	$100	$150
97	Mercedes saloon; battery-powered	Ichiko Kogyo	Japan	1960s	$175	$240
98	'Hot Rod' battery-operated car	Nomura	Japan	1950s	$140	$200
99	'Willie the Walking Car'; battery-operated	Nomura	Japan	1960s	$200	$275
100	Battery-powered 'old-time' car	Unknown	Japan	1970s	$50	$70
101	Fire engine and trailer; friction-drive	GAMA	Germany	1950s	$100	$140
102	'Cabrio 359' clockwork saloon/open tourer	Kellermann	Germany	1950s	$175	$225
103	'Rollo Series' VW 'Beetle'; friction-drive	Kellermann	Germany	1950s-1960s	$35	$50
104	Electric-powered saloon car	Kellermann	Germany	1950s-1960s	$25	$45
105	Friction-drive Citroën car	Tipp & Co	Germany	1960s	$125	$160
106	'OK Biscuits' clockwork van	Mettoy	UK	1950s	$375	$475
107	Three small clockwork vans	Wells-Brimtoy	UK	1950s-1960s	$25	$40
108	Clockwork tractor	Mettoy	UK	1950s	$40	$65
109	Boxed Minic set	Tri-ang	UK	1950s	$300	$450
110	Minic breakdown truck; clockwork	Tri-ang	UK	1950s	$140	$185
111	Minic garbage truck; clockwork	Tri-ang	UK	1950s	$100	$140
112	Minic traction engine; clockwork	Tri-ang	UK	1950s	$100	$140
113	Minic boat transporter	Tri-ang	UK	1950s	$140	$190
114	Large-scale metal pick-up truck	Buddy L	USA	1960s	$40	$60
115	San Francisco cable car; friction-drive		Taiwan	1970s	$85	$135
116	'Highway Express' friction-drive bus	Nomura	Japan	1960s-1970s	$50	$75
117	Bus	Chad Valley	UK	1950s	$250	$325
118	Motorcycle; clockwork	Tipp & Co	Germany	1950s	$275	$350
119-120	Motorcycles (AA and clown versions); clockwork	Mettoy	UK	1950s	$90	$135
121	'Motodrill Clown' motorcycle; clockwork	Schuco	Germany	1950s	$140	$185
122	'Curvo' motorcycle; clockwork	Schuco	Germany	1950s	$175	$240
123	'Mac' motorcycle; clockwork	Arnold	Germany	1940s-1950s	$600	$800
124	'Carl' motorcycle; clockwork	Schuco	Germany	1950s	$100	$150
125	Clown and motorcycle; clockwork	Toplay	Japan	1960s	$125	$175
126	Messerschmitt 'Kabin Cruiser'	Bandai	Japan	1950s	$400	$500

SHIPS, BOATS AND AIRCRAFT

127	Clockwork liner	Arnold	Germany	1950s	$300	$375
128	'Bluebird II' speedboat; clockwork	Sutcliffe	UK	1950s	$100	$150
129	'Miss England' speedboat; steam engine	Victory	UK	1950s	$75	$115
130	'Hawk' speedboat; clockwork	Sutcliffe	UK	1970s	$50	$80
131	'Neptune' tugboat; battery-powered	MT	Japan	1950s	$85	$140
132	'Pirate Ship'; battery-powered	Masudaya	Japan	1960s	$110	$165
133	'Pop-pop' boat	Unknown	India	Current	—	
134	'Pop-pop' boat	Unknown	Japan	Current	—	
135	'Pop-pop' boat	Unknown	Pakistan	Current	—	
136	'Pop-pop' boat	Unknown	Japan	Current	—	
137	Ocean liner; battery-powered	MT	Japan	1960s	$100	$165
138	'SS Silver Mariner'; battery-operated	Unknown	Japan	1950s-1960s	$125	$180
139	'Submarino'; battery-powered	Schuco	Germany	1960s-1970s	$85	$130
140	'Nautilus' submarine; friction-drive	Unknown	UK	1950s	$100	$140
141	'The Nautilus' submarine; clockwork	Sutcliffe	UK	1950s	$200	$275
142	'Supersonic Boeing 733'; battery-powered	—	China	1970s-1980s	$50	$75

dition standards. This is one collecting category where the smart collector buys nothing graded less than "excellent". If you find a toy that does not meet your standards, keep searching. Before you know it, you will find one that does.

Ideally, buy only toys that have their original box. The original box, assuming it is in fine condition or better, adds an additional fifty to one hundred percent to the value of the toy in "fine" condition. Learn to grade the toy and box separately. Just because a toy is in excellent condition does not mean that its box is as well. Any box below fine condition must be discounted heavily.

For a detailed understanding of the American toy market and the forces that drive it, consult Harry L. Rinker's *Collector's Guide To Toys, Games, and Puzzles*, published by Wallace Homestead Book Company in 1991.

The ranges given in the price guide that follows are for a toy in fine condition (C6 on the standard American grading scale) and excellent condition (C8 on the standard American grading scale). Fine means that the toy shows some wear in spots, has been well taken care of by its owner, and is presentable for display purposes. Excellent means that the toy has only minor wear along its edges. The values exclude the box.

Owners of postwar tin toys played with them. As a result, few survive in

143 'Turboprop Jet'; battery-powered	Yoneya	Japan	1960s	$150	$225
144 'Pan-Am Skyway Helicopter'; friction-drive	Daiya	Japan	1960s	$90	$140
145 'Bombardier Prop Fighter Plane'; battery-powered	WACO	Japan	1960s	$65	$110
146- 'Elektro Radiant' Viscount airliner; battery-	Schuco	Germany	1957-1968	$250	$400
147 powered (Lufthansa and BOAC liveries)					
148 'Air France' airliner; clockwork	Joustra	France	1950s	$200	$275
149 'Jet Airliner'; battery-powered	—	China	1960s	$50	$75
150 'Air Plane'; friction-drive	—	China	Current	—	
151 'Training Plane'; clockwork	—	China	Current	—	

TOY AND MODEL TRAINS

152 'No 50' O-gage tender-locomotive and rolling stock, clockwork	Hornby	UK	1950s	$100	$150
153 'M1' O-gage loco and tender set; clockwork	Hornby	UK	1950s	$100	$150
154 'Pullman' coach	Hornby	UK	1950s	$25	$35
155 'No 40 Tank Locomotive'; O-gage, clockwork	Hornby	UK	1950s	$50	$80
156 Track toy featuring railroad theme	Arnold	Germany	1940s-50s	$130	$180
157 'Prince Charles' locomotive; clockwork	Bassett-Lowke	UK	1950s	$200	$275
158 O-gage train set; clockwork	Mettoy	UK	1950s	$85	$140
159 'Eton' locomotive and tender set; O-gage, clockwork	Mettoy	UK	1950s	$125	$175
160 'Pullman' coach from 'Eton' boxed set	Mettoy	UK	1950s	$20	$30
161 'Tinkling Locomotive'; battery-powered	Masutoku	Japan	1960s	$45	$75
162 'Atchison, Topeka & Santa Fe' novelty train	Yoneya	Japan	1960s-1970s	$25	$40

ROBOTS AND SPACE TOYS

163 'Space Tank'; battery-powered	Nomura	Japan	1960s	$175	$250
164 'Space Tank'; battery-powered	—	China	1970s	$85	$130
165 Rocketship; clockwork	Unknown	Unknown	1950s	$225	$350
166 'Pioneer' spaceship; clockwork	Kanto	Japan	1950s	$200	$300
167 'Space Port' track toy	Technofix	Germany	1950s-1960s	$225	$325
168 Flying saucer; friction-drive	Unknown	Japan	1960s	$80	$140
169 Flying saucer; friction-drive	—	China	Current	$50	$75
170 'Space Station'; friction-drive	Unknown	Japan	1960s-1970s	$275	$350
171 Space ship; friction-drive	Wells-Brimtoy	UK	1950s	$80	$140
172 'Holdauto' space vehicle; battery-powered	Lemavar Gyar	Hungary	1980s	$100	$150
173 'Dino Robot'; battery-powered	Unknown	Japan	1960s	$650	$800
174 Robot; clockwork	Unknown	Japan	1950s-1960s	$175	$225
175 'Space Walk Man'; battery-powered	—	China	Current	—	
176- Limited-edition ceramic copies of rare post-	—	UK	1980	$40	$65
178 war Japanese robots					
179 Robot; battery-operated	Unknown	Japan	1960s-1970s	$85	$145
180 'Doctor Who Dalek'; clockwork	Cowan de Groot	UK	1950s-1960s	$300	$450
181 Trade leaflet featuring 'Shogun' figures	Bullmark	Japan	1950s-1960s	—	

PRESENT-DAY REISSUES OF POST-WAR TIN TOYS

182 Clockwork merry-go-round; replica of Blomer & Schüler toy	—	China	Current	$75	$125
183 Mechanical rowing boat; replica	Paya	Spain	Current	$50	$75
184- Replicas of Schuco 'Oldtimer' series of	GAMA	Germany	Current	—	
188 clockwork cars					
189 Replica of Schuco 'Akustico 2002' clockwork car	GAMA	Germany	Current	—	
190 Replica of Schuco 'Examico 4001' clockwork car	GAMA	Germany	Current	—	
191 Replica of Schuco 'Studio' Mercedes racing car; clockwork	GAMA	Germany	Current	—	

OTHER TINPLATE TOYS

192 Track toy featuring racing car theme; clockwork	Technofix	Germany	1960s	$85	$140
193 'Country Tour' track toy; clockwork	Technofix	Germany	1960s	$145	$200
194 Track toy	Arnold	Germany	1950s	$100	$150
195 'Local Shuttle' track toy; clockwork	Unknown	India	Current	—	
196 House and garage	Mettoy	UK	1950s-1960s	$60	$95
197 Bungalow	Marx	USA	1950s	$45	$75
198 'General Hospital'	Mettoy	UK	1950s-1960s	$75	$115
199 Fire-station set; clockwork	Mettoy	UK	1950s	$120	$175
200 'Merry Builders' sand toy	Cowan de Groot	UK	1950s	$75	$120
201 'Batman Hoop-la Game'	Lone Star	UK	1966	$125	$175
202 Cowboy shooting game	Unknown	UK	1950s	$100	$150
203 Gorilla shooting game	Nomura	Japan	1950s	$150	$200
204 Batman gun	Tada	Japan	1960s	$650	$800
205- Clacker toys	T Conn	USA	1950s	$14	$20
206					
207 'Orbitoy'	Dunbee-Combex	UK	1960s	$35	$60
208 Batman and Robin spinning top	Unknown	Unknown	1960s	$35	$50
209 Clockwork gramophone	GAMA	Germany	1950s	$120	$165
210 Typewriter	Mettoy	UK	1960s	$40	$60

mint or near mint condition. Both terms are heavily abused in the tin toy market. Collectors and dealers alike have a bad habit of overgrading their toys. Few "mint" and "near mint" toys can stand close scrutiny. It is for this reason that excellent was used as the upper level of the price ranges presented.

Do not be misled by the above. It is not meant to discourage you from collecting postwar tin toys. Its purpose is to put you on alert so that your collecting experience is a positive one.

Finally, remember that what you are collecting are toys. There is no fun if all they do is sit on a shelf or in a display case. Oh, go ahead! Take them out and play with them.

Index

PICTURE CREDITS

Many of the photographs in this book illustrate items in the collections listed below. All other toys illustrated are in private collections. Note that the numbers refer to picture/caption numbers and not page numbers.

Graham Barlow; *collector of Popeye and other tin toys:* 1, 34, 46, 48, 49, 70, 80, 81, 98, 127.

Richard Clark; *trades as 'Tin Town Toys', Leicester:* 13, 133, 134, 135, 136, 151, 169, 175, 195.

Christine and John Hopkinson; *Haworth Museum of Childhood:* 67, 87, 100, 107, 117, 141, 152, 153, 154, 155, 157, 158, 159, 160, 163, 170, 196, 197, 198, 210.

Hattie and Ross Hutchinson; *The Incredibly Fantastic Toy Show, Lincoln:* 2, 3, 14, 32, 52, 54, 57, 62, 71, 82, 85, 97, 101, 102, 115, 130, 131, 137, 138, 139, 142, 144, 149, 150, 164, 166, 171, 172, 173, 174, 179, 182, 199.

Ed Kelly; *collector of Batman associated toys:* 18, 19, 20, 21, 22, 23, 24, 25, 26, 27, 201, 204, 208.

Frank Nelson; *collector, automata-maker, and toy restorer:* 6, 7, 15, 35, 37, 39, 44, 45, 50, 51, 59, 63, 91, 125, 129, 140, 167, 168, 183, 194, 200, 202, 207.

Jim Whittaker; *collector of model railroads and novelty toys:* 17, 29, 30, 61, 88, 95, 96, 99, 103, 105, 106, 161, 162.